Great
Cartoonists

Craig E. Blohm

ReferencePoint
Press®

San Diego, CA

About the Author
Craig E. Blohm has written numerous books and magazine articles for
young readers. He and his wife, Desiree, reside in Tinley Park, Illinois.

© 2017 ReferencePoint Press, Inc.
Printed in the United States

For more information, contact:
ReferencePoint Press, Inc.
PO Box 27779
San Diego, CA 92198
www.ReferencePointPress.com

Picture Credits:

Cover: Depositphotos.com
 6: Photofest
10: Photofest
15: Photofest
20: Associated Press
25: © Nancy Kaszerman/ZUMA Press/Corbis
31: David Cooper/Toronto Star/ZUMA Press/Newscom

37: Rick Mackler/ZUMA Press/Newscom
41: © Universal Pictures/Photofest
45: 20th Century Fox TV/Album/Newscom
52: Jean Nelson/Depositphotos.com
57: Fox/Photofest
63: Associated Press
67: Cartoon Network/Photofest

LIBRARY OF CONGRESS CATALOGING-IN-PUBLICATION DATA

Names: Blohm, Craig E., 1948- author.
Title: Great cartoonists / by Craig E. Blohm.
Description: San Diego, CA : ReferencePoint Press, Inc., 2017. | Series:
   Collective biographies | Includes bibliographical references and index.
Identifiers: LCCN 2016004760 (print) | LCCN 2016005277 (ebook) | ISBN
   9781601529961 (hardback) | ISBN 9781601529978 (eBook)
Subjects: LCSH: Cartoonists--United States--Biography--Juvenile literature. |
   Cartoonists--Canada--Biography--Juvenile literature.
Classification: LCC NC1305 .B49 2016 (print) | LCC NC1305 (ebook) | DDC
   741.5/69730922--dc23
LC record available at http://lccn.loc.gov/2016004760

CONTENTS

INTRODUCTION The Art of the Cartoonist

I n today's culture, many colorful characters have attained star status in the popular media. In the movies, Batman fights crime on the dark streets of Gotham City, and Superman soars through the skies, protecting the innocent people below from falling airliners and supervillains. On television, a rascal named Bart Simpson constantly befuddles the adults around him. And every year, a round-headed boy named Charlie Brown learns the true meaning of Christmas, even though he never learns that trying to kick a football held by his pint-sized nemesis, Lucy, is not a very good idea.

All of these characters, and countless more, originated in the imaginations of the artists who brought them to life: the cartoonists. "Comic art is an art form in itself," writes Alex Raymond, creator of the comic *Flash Gordon*. "A comic artist begins with a white sheet of paper and dreams up the whole business—he is playwright, director, editor, and artist at once."[1]

See You in the Funny Papers

In the late nineteenth and early twentieth centuries, before radio, television, and the Internet were invented, people got the latest information about the world from newspapers. Although the news published in the daily or weekly papers included stories of crime, wars, and human suffering, these grim reports were balanced by lighter fare, including comics. Between 1895 and 1898, a comic called *The Yellow Kid* ran in two New York newspapers, arguably making it the first comic strip in America. As the twentieth century unfolded, comics grew as popular entertainment for the masses. Soon newspapers featured an entire color section of comics in their Sunday editions. By the 1920s, "See you in the funny papers" became a fashionable saying when bidding a friend farewell, an acknowledgment that life can sometimes be as crazy as the comics.

The Evolving Cartoon

As comics grew in popularity, the strips appearing in funny papers began to broaden their horizons. By the 1920s and 1930s, comics had evolved from showing simple humor to portraying action, adventure, and enough romance to rival the radio soap operas of the day. Comic strips featuring space traveler Buck Rogers and jungle hero Tarzan debuted on the same day in 1929. Cartoonist Chester Gould introduced square-jawed Dick Tracy, the first comic strip detective, in 1931. Aviation became a popular subject as well, with Hal Forrest's *Tailspin Tommy*, Zack Mosley's *Smilin' Jack*, and Milton Caniff's *Terry and the Pirates*.

World War II spurred several war-themed comics, including *Willie and Joe*, about two war-weary soldiers who symbolized the ordinary American in combat. Their creator, Bill Mauldin, himself a sergeant, won a Pulitzer Prize for his single-panel drawings, which often disparaged officers while showing empathy for the enlisted soldier. As the nation returned to normal after the war, comics looked toward entertaining their audience with zany characters and relatable family situations. Strips such as *Peanuts*, debuting in 1950,

> "A comic artist begins with a white sheet of paper and dreams up the whole business—he is playwright, director, editor, and artist at once."[1]
>
> —*Alex Raymond, cartoonist.*

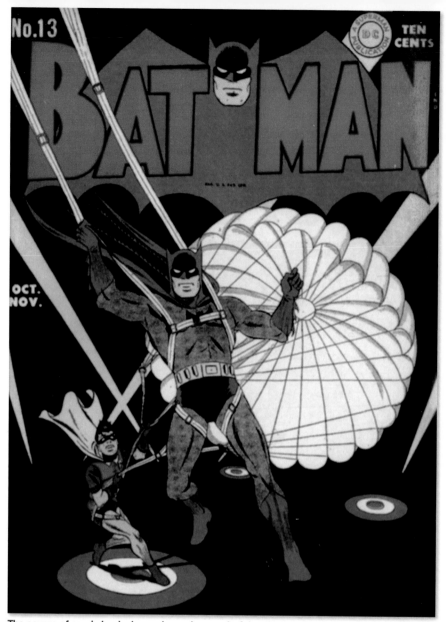

The covers of comic books have always been colorful and attractive. The images of costumed superheroes battling villains or of cartoon characters in comedic situations showcase an artist's style and his or her ability to entice readers to eagerly consume the story within.

and *Hi and Lois*, which began in 1954, were typical comics of the early postwar decades. By the 1970s and 1980s, the hapless Viking warrior Hagar the Horrible, the corporate cubicle worker Dilbert, and the lasagna-loving feline Garfield all brought laughs to appreciative audiences.

Cartoons as Social Statements

While most cartoons use humor to great effect, strips can deal with serious issues as well. Garry Trudeau's *Doonesbury* regularly skewers politics and war and has tackled such controversial subjects as abortion. *Prickly City*, originally drawn by Chicago cartoonist Scott Stantis, examines politics from a conservative viewpoint. *Funky Winkerbean* by Tom Batiuk has dealt with drug abuse, bullying, and teenage pregnancy. In 2007 the strip concluded a long-running story with the death of a character who had waged a brave battle with breast cancer. Many readers were angry that a comic would portray such a serious matter on the funny pages and vowed never to read *Funky Winkerbean* again.

> "Cartoon art, a truly democratic art for a democratic society, has always played a special role in America. Cartoons have helped spark revolutions, sway election campaigns, reveal corruption, and promote reform."[2]
>
> —James Billington, former Librarian of Congress.

The fact that a comic strip can elicit such a response underscores the power that cartoonists have to bring both laughter and drama to a mass audience. Perhaps the best statement about the importance of cartoons is by James Billington, the former Librarian of Congress. In a book celebrating 250 years of cartooning in America, Billington writes:

> Cartoon art, a truly democratic art for a democratic society, has always played a special role in America. Cartoons have helped spark revolutions, sway election campaigns, reveal corruption, and promote reform. They educate and entertain, inform and enlighten. Artful or awful, they are the graphic snapshots of our times, spontaneous and accessible to all.[2]

That may seem like a tall order for simple characters made of ink lines on paper, but the talented cartoonists who hold the pen have always risen to, and often above, the challenge.

CHAPTER 1

Charles Schulz

When his kindergarten teacher handed out crayons and paper and told the class to draw whatever came to mind, the neatly dressed little boy knew just what his subject would be. To illustrate the fierce Minnesota winters he knew so well, he drew a man shoveling mounds of snow. Then, letting his imagination run wild, the boy added a tropical palm tree to the wintry scene. When the teacher saw his drawing, she said, "Someday, Charles, you're going to be an artist."[3] Charles Schulz would ultimately fulfill his teacher's prophecy with a career that spanned fifty years of cartooning and produced the most beloved comic strip of all time.

The Early Years of "Sparky" Schulz

Charles Monroe Schulz was born in Minneapolis, Minnesota, on November 26, 1922, the only child of Carl and Dena Schulz. Soon after his birth, an uncle—apparently seeing in the infant some resemblance to a popular comic strip horse named Spark Plug—nicknamed him "Sparky." For the rest of his life, Schulz was Sparky to his family and close friends.

Sparky's father was a barber with a shop in St. Paul, where the family moved in 1927. Sparky often visited the shop, and at the end of the workday father and son walked home, talking about the newspaper comics they had read. Carl was an avid fan of the comics, and on weekends, when the Sunday papers with their color funny pages came out, he pored over the comic sections of four newspapers. Father and son's mutual love of the comics reinforced Sparky's interest in one day having his work appear in the funny papers.

In grammar school, Schulz's teachers considered him an exceptional student and skipped him ahead the equivalent of a full grade. The promotion meant that Schulz would spend the rest of his school years competing with classmates who were older and taller than he was. The result was a self-conscious, lonely, and insecure boy who worried about every-

> "All the way through school I could draw better [than] or as well as anyone in the class."[4]
>
> —Charles Schulz

thing. The one area that he excelled in was drawing. "All the way through school," Schulz commented, "I could draw better [than] or as well as anyone in the class."[4] That talent would eventually give Sparky Schulz the career that he had always dreamed of.

Becoming Professional

By the time he entered St. Paul's Central High School, Schulz was a shy teen who concentrated on perfecting his drawing skills while other boys were beginning to discover girls. "I never regard-ed myself as being good-looking," Schulz recalled, "and I never had a date in high school, because I thought, who'd want to date me?"[5] Sitting at the dining room table, Schulz copied comic strips from the St. Paul newspapers, drawing on whatever paper he could find around the house. When he was fourteen years old, he sent a drawing to a newspaper feature called *Ripley's Believe It or Not!*, which illustrated odd and remarkable facts. Schulz's submission was a drawing of his dog, Spike, a black-and-white mutt who had the habit of eating strange things. On February 22, 1937, the drawing appeared with the caption "A hunting dog

that eats pins, tacks and razor blades," and the byline "Drawn by 'Sparky.'" Schulz was now a published cartoonist.

Schulz managed barely passing grades in high school. In his senior year, an art teacher asked him to draw some cartoons for the yearbook. He excitedly drew and submitted several cartoons. But when the book came out, Schulz discovered that his drawings were not there. "To this day," Schulz recalled, "I have no idea why they were rejected."[6] The rejection stung, but did not discourage the budding cartoonist.

Art School and the Army

One day, Schulz's mother saw an advertisement for a correspondence art course from the Federal School of Applied Cartooning. "Do you like to draw?" read the ad. "Send in for our free talent test."[7] Schulz enrolled and dutifully completed each lesson that was mailed to his home. He learned new pen and ink skills, human anatomy, and techniques for drawing children, receiving critiques from the school's staff by return mail.

Schulz graduated from the Federal School on December 1, 1941, less than a week before the United States entered World War II. Drafted into the army in 1943, Schulz had not only the war to worry about, but a personal tragedy as well. Dena, his mother, had suffered for years with cancer. By the time Schulz had to leave for basic training, she was gravely ill. "Good-bye, Sparky," she said from her sickbed. "We'll probably never see each other again."[8] Schulz left to report for duty; the next day, Dena passed away. In one day, Sparky's safe and familiar life had turned upside down.

Schulz spent two years in the army, attaining the rank of staff sergeant. After a tour in France and Germany, he came home in August 1945. He had survived the war and earned a Combat Infantryman Badge, the symbol of action in combat. Back in St. Paul he could now concentrate on becoming the professional cartoonist he aspired to be.

Breaking In

Schulz's first professional cartooning job was not quite what he expected. He was hired by the editor of *Topix*, a comic magazine published by the Catholic Church, to letter dialogue for cartoons drawn by other artists. Although it was the lowest rung on the cartooning ladder, it was a start. What really excited Schulz, however, was the editor's promise to publish *Just Keep Laughing*, a strip that Schulz had been drawing in his spare time. Not that he had much time to spare: He was also working as an instructor at the Federal School, renamed Art Instruction, Inc., to review and grade students' work.

Frank Wing, a coworker at the school, saw samples of *Just Keep Laughing* and was impressed. "Sparky," he said, "I think you should draw more of those little kids. They are pretty good."[9] Schulz took the advice and refined the strip's concept, eliminating adult characters and focusing on the children. Schulz submitted

Ice Skating in California

When Schulz moved to California in 1958, he left behind something that had been a part of his life in the frigid Minnesota winters. Ice skating had been the winter sport of choice for Minnesota children, and few backyards did not have a makeshift rink for skating and ice hockey.

The Redwood Empire Ice Arena in Santa Rosa was Schulz's little slice of Minnesota in the northern California sunshine. The $2 million project, spearheaded by his wife, Joyce, was completed in 1969. Its architectural style is that of a Swiss chalet, surrounded by towering redwoods that give the area the feeling of an alpine forest. The Redwood Arena boasts a regulation-size rink, a restaurant called the Warm Puppy Café, and a studio where Schulz worked.

Also known as Snoopy's Home Ice, the arena hosts skating and youth and adult hockey leagues and offers skating lessons. It also holds the annual Snoopy's Senior World Hockey Tournament, in which Schulz played every year until his death in 2000. "Playing hockey is one of the few things that takes my mind completely off everything else in my life," Schulz said. "You don't have time to think of anything else."

Inside the Warm Puppy Café is a table that remains unoccupied. Preserved under its glass top are photographs of Schulz's life and work. The table stands forever reserved for the creator of the characters whose images fill the arena and the hearts of all those who skate there.

Quoted in M. Thomas Inge, ed., *Charles M. Schulz: Conversations.* Jackson: University Press of Mississippi, 2000, p. 81.

---

his new comic, called *Li'l Folks*, to the Minneapolis newspapers the *Star* and *Tribune*. The editors liked the strip but could not guarantee Schulz a regular space in the paper, so he took samples to rival newspaper the *St. Paul Pioneer Press*. On June 22, 1947, *Li'l Folks* began appearing in the *Pioneer Press*'s women's section.

From *Li'l Folks* to *Peanuts*

Schulz eventually tired of seeing his creation on the women's page instead of in the funny pages with the rest of the comics. When his editors refused to change the location of the strip, he left the paper. But Schulz did not give up. "In the spring of 1950," he recalled, "I took all the best [*Li'l Folks*] cartoons I had done for the *Pioneer Press* and redrew them and submitted them to United Feature Syndicate. They liked them enough to ask if I'd care to come to New York to talk about it."[10]

In New York, United Feature's editorial director praised the strip's "charm, its characters, its style of humor."[11] Schulz received a five-year contract with the syndicate, which would market *Li'l Folks* to newspapers around the country. Schulz was thrilled with all but one aspect of the deal. Because of other comics bearing similar names, the title *Li'l Folks* could not be used. Without Schulz's consent, the strip was renamed *Peanuts*. Schulz felt the new title trivialized his characters, but he had no power to overturn the syndicate's decision. For the rest of his life, Schulz regarded the name *Peanuts* as "the worst title ever thought of for a comic strip."[12]

Peanuts Begins

Despite Schulz's displeasure with the new name, the first *Peanuts* comic was published in seven newspapers on October 2, 1950. The strip consisted of four panels featuring a boy named Charlie Brown and his young companions. The inaugural strip shows Charlie Brown walking down the street past two other children, Patty and Shermy. "Here comes good ol' Charlie Brown," Patty says. Shermy echoes her words until the last panel, in which he declares, "How I hate him!"[13] From this beginning, it was clear *Peanuts* would be a different kind of comic strip. Cartoonist Garry Trudeau notes that Schulz "completely revolutionized the art form, deepening it, filling it with possibility, giving permission to all who followed to write from the heart and intellect."[14]

> "[Charles Schulz] completely revolutionized the art form, deepening it, filling it with possibility, giving permission to all who followed to write from the heart and intellect."[14]
>
> —*Garry Trudeau, cartoonist.*

Schulz drew *Peanuts* in a minimalist style. The detailed environments that appeared in most comics were replaced by a single horizon line, leaving generous white space for the children, who were drawn with simple pen strokes. After creating a pencil rough,

Schulz lettered the dialogue first, then inked in the characters, never employing assistants as other cartoonists often did, and still do. Schulz made Charlie Brown the embodiment of his own apprehensive personality. "I worry about almost all there is in life to worry about," Schulz commented, "and because I worry, Charlie Brown has to worry."[15] Schulz was most content when drawing his strip, saying, "It is one of the few situations in my life where I feel totally secure. When I sit behind the drawing board I feel that I am in command."[16]

Schulz took the names for many of his characters from people he knew. Patty was named after Schulz's cousin, and Shermy was his childhood friend, Sherman Plepler. Charlie Brown was named after Charles Brown, a fellow instructor at Art Instruction. It was while working at the school that Schulz met two women who would influence his life.

Sparky in Love

The army had given Schulz a new confidence in himself. No longer an awkward teenager, Schulz now set his sights on a young woman at Art Instruction. Donna Johnson was a pretty, red-haired twenty-one-year-old working in the school's accounting office. In February 1950 Schulz asked her for a date, and they saw each other often for several months. But Johnson was also dating a man named Alan Wold and was uncertain as to which suitor she would marry. Johnson eventually made her decision, becoming Mrs. Alan Wold in October. Crushed by the rejection, Schulz later commented, "I can think of no more emotionally damaging loss than to be turned down by someone you love very much."[17] The incident inspired the creation of the Little Red-Haired Girl, a character for whose affections Charlie Brown pines, but never wins. Appropriately, she is spoken of but never seen.

The next year, Schulz met Joyce Halverson, the sister of another art school coworker. A lively woman whose husband had abandoned her and her infant daughter, Meredith, Halverson took a liking to the mild-mannered cartoonist. The feeling was mutual, and they were married on April 18, 1951. Over the course of their twenty-one-year marriage, the Schulzes added sons Monte and Craig and daughters Amy and Jill to their family. Divorced in 1972, Schulz married Elizabeth Jean "Jeannie" Clyde the next year, a union that would last until his death in 2000.

Schulz continued to improve *Peanuts*, adding new characters and drawing a more detailed environment for them. By now, people were beginning to take notice of Charlie Brown and his gang.

The World Meets Charlie Brown

From its modest beginning, *Peanuts* grew to become one of the most successful comic strips of all time. By 1958, more than 350 US and 40 foreign papers carried the strip, and the number kept climbing. That same year, the Schulz clan left Minnesota for the sunny climate of California. *Peanuts* now included the cast of characters so familiar today to millions of readers. Lucy van Pelt

Charlie Brown and Snoopy have become icons for young and old alike. While they began their lives in newspaper strips, today they are seen on greeting cards, toys, clothes, and other merchandise. Here, the pair appear on a 2002 television special, A Charlie Brown Valentine.

became Charlie Brown's nemesis, constantly proclaiming Charlie a "blockhead." Linus, Lucy's little brother, carried a security blanket wherever he went, experiencing fits of anxiety if he and his blanket were separated. Charlie Brown's beagle, Snoopy, lived a vivid fantasy life as a World War I flying ace, a novelist, college student Joe Cool, an astronaut, and many more imaginary personas.

The world of *Peanuts* spread beyond the newspaper comic pages. Books reprinting the strips became popular, as did *Peanuts* toys, games, greeting cards, and apparel. In 1965 *A Charlie Brown Christmas* aired on CBS, the first of more than forty *Peanuts* television specials, many of which are still broadcast annually. In 1967 a musical entitled *You're a Good Man, Charlie*

The Gospel According to Sparky

When Charles Schulz agreed to write *A Charlie Brown Christmas*, he had one non-negotiable demand: a scene of Linus reading the Nativity story from the Bible could not be deleted. As a man of faith, Schulz wanted to present the true biblical message, resisting television's trend toward nonspiritual Christmas programs.

As a young man, Schulz attended the Church of God and, later, the United Methodist Church. He taught Sunday school and studied scripture, making copious notes in his personal Bible. By his own account, he was the first cartoonist to put Bible verses and theological themes into a comic strip. In *Peanuts*, Linus was usually the one to take on the deep theological questions. From 1956 to 1965 Schulz drew a comic for the Church of God's *Youth* magazine. Entitled *Young Pillars*, the single-panel strip's gentle teasing of church life was directed toward a teenage audience. In 1965 theology student Robert L. Short wrote a best-selling book, *The Gospel According to Peanuts*, using *Peanuts* strips to explain Christianity.

Later in his life, Schulz's personal theology went through changes. He once said, "I think the best theology is no theology," seemingly identifying himself as a secular humanist. Some even called him an atheist. But he was neither; Schulz's faith ran deeper than mere labels. For him, faith lived inside a person, not necessarily inside the walls of a church. And the expression of that faith can even come from the mouths of cartoon characters.

Quoted in Stephen J. Lind, *A Charlie Brown Religion: Exploring the Spiritual Life and Work of Charles M. Schulz*. Jackson: University Press of Mississippi, 2015, p. 180.

Brown, began a four-year run in New York. In 2015, the gang hit the big screen in *The Peanuts Movie*, a computer-animated, 3-D film written by Schulz's son Craig and grandson Bryan.

The Longest Story

As the lives of his characters continued to delight readers, Schulz's own life became challenged by health issues. He underwent open heart surgery in 1981, subsequently suffering a tremor in his hand that made drawing difficult. Aware that his declining health would no longer allow him to keep up the rigorous schedule of a daily and Sunday strip, Schulz decided to retire.

Peanuts eventually appeared in twenty-six hundred newspapers, with an audience of some 355 million readers. In nearly fifty years, Sparky had drawn 17,897 *Peanuts* strips, "arguably the longest story ever told by a single artist in human history,"[18] according to popular culture professor Robert Thompson. His influence can still be seen in such strips as *Doonesbury*, *Garfield*, and *Bloom County*. Since 2002, Schulz's vast body of work has been preserved in the Charles M. Schulz Museum and Research Center in Santa Rosa, California.

Schulz died at age seventy-seven on February 12, 2000. The next day the last *Peanuts* strip appeared in the Sunday newspapers. It was a single panel containing familiar images of the *Peanuts* gang and Schulz's farewell to his readers, which he had composed two months earlier:

> "[*Peanuts* is] arguably the longest story ever told by a single artist in human history."[18]
>
> —Professor Robert Thompson

> I have been fortunate to draw Charlie Brown and his friends for almost 50 years. . . . My family does not wish Peanuts to be continued by anyone else, therefore I am announcing my retirement. . . . Charlie Brown, Snoopy, Linus, Lucy. . . how can I ever forget them.[19]

If his readers could reply, surely they would say, "Charlie Schulz, how can we ever forget you?"

CHAPTER 2

Garry Trudeau

On a dusty roadside in Iraq, medics attend an army lieutenant who lies gravely wounded on a stretcher, his leg shattered. It is April 2004 and the second Iraq war is raging. The soldier's Humvee had been patrolling near Fallujah when it was ambushed by insurgents firing rocket-propelled grenades. While awaiting evacuation after the attack, the wounded soldier's friend Ray encourages him to fight for his life: "You're not dying here, man! Not today!"[20]

The lieutenant did not die, but the loss of his leg meant months of grueling physical and psychological therapy. His experience was not unlike thousands of other soldiers wounded in Iraq, with one exception: he was a character in a comic strip. Known only as B.D., his injury, rehabilitation, and eventual recovery was chronicled in the strip *Doonesbury*, written and drawn by cartoonist Garry Trudeau. It was not the first time a provocative topic was covered by Trudeau, and it would not be the last.

Early Life

Garretson Beekman "Garry" Trudeau was born in New York City on July 21, 1948, the only son of Jean and Dr. Francis Trudeau

Jr. His father founded the Trudeau Institute, a medical research facility in Saranac Lake, New York, and moved his family to the affluent upstate community when Garry was five years old. Trudeau remembers his youth in Saranac Lake as "an idyllic, Huckleberry [Finn] existence—fishing, tree houses, and little adult supervision."[21] In addition to these typical youthful activities, Trudeau's artistic side began to emerge in the area of theater. When he was seven years old, he started writing plays and staging them in his basement, an activity that he would continue for years.

After his parents divorced in 1960, Trudeau was sent to St. Paul's School, a college preparatory boarding school in Concord, New Hampshire. At St. Paul's, Trudeau pursued art, becoming president of the school's Art Association and winning the senior-class art prize. He did not yet consider cartooning as a career. "Newspaper comics were generally unavailable to me in boarding school," Trudeau recalls, "so I had few early influences. I was a dabbler. I thought my path would be in theater or fine art."[22] But it would be cartoons that emerged from his artistic talent. His first cartoon was "Weenie Man," a character Trudeau drew for posters promoting the sale of hot dogs at St. Paul's football games. Trudeau describes how the character would "solve vexing problems by literally tossing hot dogs at them. . . . The six episodic posters featuring Weenie Man gave me that first little buzz of peer recognition, something I could build on."[23] He would continue to build his career path in college.

> "Newspaper comics were generally unavailable to me in boarding school, so I had few early influences. I was a dabbler. I thought my path would be in theater or fine art."[22]
>
> —*Garry Trudeau*

Bull Tales at Yale

In 1966 Trudeau entered Yale University in New Haven, Connecticut. Majoring in graphic arts, he became the editor of the university's humor magazine, the *Yale Record,* and wrote for the campus newspaper, the *Yale Daily News*. He also began drawing a comic strip named *Bull Tales*, taking its title from the Yale bulldog

Garry Trudeau is an artist that seeks to entertain yet is not afraid to confront pressing social issues. His strip *Doonesbury*, which began in 1970, after his graduation from Yale (where this photo was taken), remained relevant to readers by tackling such controversial topics as the US war in Vietnam, prejudice, homosexuality, and unemployment.

mascot. Trudeau's idea for *Bull Tales* was inspired by Yale football player Brian Dowling, the college's star quarterback. Dowling became B.D. in the strip, a "knuckleheaded college quarterback,"[24] who was never seen without his football helmet.

The strip was a crudely drawn but humorous look at college life. In 1968 Trudeau showed samples of *Bull Tales* to Reed Hundt, editor of the *Yale Daily News*, hoping he would accept them for publication. Hundt looked at the strips and said, "They're all right. We publish pretty much anything."[25] On September 30, 1968, *Bull Tales* began running in the Yale paper. Within two months the strip's combination of biting satire and familiar campus setting had gained popularity with the Yale students. Then, on November 28, Trudeau received a letter that changed his life.

Considering Syndication

The letter was from John B. Kennedy, a partner at the Universal Press Syndicate in New York City. It read, in part, "I have noticed your cartoon panel *Bull Tales* in the *Yale Daily News* and think it is very clever. I was wondering if I could see other samples of your work with a possible view to future syndication."[26] It was an amazing offer for a fledgling cartoonist whose first strip had appeared for only two months in a college newspaper. Trudeau, like most college-age males at the time, faced an uncertain future due to the possibility of being drafted for the Vietnam War. He hesitated in taking Kennedy's offer, but the next summer Trudeau visited the syndicate's office in New York. He was surprised to learn that the Universal Press Syndicate was a small, part-time venture run by two men, James Andrews (who used the pseudonym John B. Kennedy to protect his full-time job), and John McMeel, a sales director for another syndicate.

Trudeau drew thirty-six sample *Bull Tales* strips to show the syndicate. But he was having some doubts about his ability to create a daily comic strip and at the same time maintain good grades at Yale. He decided to postpone syndicating his strip, telling Universal Press that he felt "it would be impossible for me to be a student and a cartoonist simultaneously and expect to be good at either."[27] By the time Trudeau graduated from Yale in June 1970, however, he was ready to move forward with syndication. He signed a twelve-year contract with Universal Press to market his strip to newspapers across the country. "At this point," Andrews told Trudeau, "the strip would be better off as non-political."[28] Fortunately, Trudeau ignored the advice.

Introducing *Doonesbury*

Trudeau began redrawing his earlier *Bull Tales* strips for the syndicate to market to a nationwide audience. But there was a problem with the name of the strip: *Bull Tales* had no meaning to anyone outside of Yale. Trudeau came up with a new title: *Doonesbury*. It was a combination of the prep school word *doone*, meaning someone who is good-natured but clueless, and the last part of Trudeau's college roommate's name, Charles Pillsbury. A character

The Certainty of Youth

For a cartoonist whose comic strip has taken on so many politicians and political themes, it would seem that Garry Trudeau has politics in his blood. Although the teenage years are usually a time of rebellion and strong opinions about almost everything, Trudeau was decidedly detached from the politics of the day, as he observes in an interview with *Rolling Stone* magazine.

> I wasn't particularly politically attuned growing up. There wasn't much debate at our dinner table. My parents were Republicans, so the GOP was my team, and Ike [President Dwight D. Eisenhower] was our genial manager. In '60, I was too young to really respond to JFK's charisma as intuitively as I was repelled by Nixon's sleaziness, and in 1964, I was so disengaged that I actually designed placards for both parties at my high school. Later I came to admire Robert Kennedy and Martin Luther King, but more as pop figures than as visionaries who changed the world. Vietnam was the wake-up call. That's when I really started paying attention, and by then heroes were in scarce supply. Besides, who needed role models? We had the certainty of youth.

Quoted in Kerry D. Soper, *Garry Trudeau: "Doonesbury" and the Aesthetics of Satire.* Jackson: University Press of Mississippi, 2008, p. 27.

named Mike in *Bull Tales* became Michael Doonesbury, the main character of the new comic strip, of whom Trudeau admits, "I'm the model for Michael."[29]

The inaugural episode of *Doonesbury* appeared in twenty-eight newspapers on October 26, 1970. In the first strip, B.D. sits in his dorm at fictional Walden College awaiting the arrival of a new, hopefully cool roommate. "Hi there!" an overexcited young man says upon entering. "My name's Mike Doonesbury. I hail from Tulsa, Oklahoma and women adore me. Glad to meet you, roomie!"[30] B.D. is not impressed and laments the bugs in the college roommate-matching computer program. Trudeau recalls that, from this "tragically inept" beginning, Mike Doonesbury slowly evolved into "the group's designated grown-up. His main job was to provide contrast, to play magnetic north as everyone around him headed south."[31]

That group eventually grew to encompass more than forty major and minor characters, including activist turned radio host Mark Slackmeyer, hippie Zonker Harris, feminist Joanie Caucus, and Barbara Ann "Boopsie" Boopstein, former cheerleader and, later, B.D.'s wife. In the early years, *Doonesbury* remained centered on the experiences of these characters, who lived in an off-campus communal house founded by Mike Doonesbury. But with its growing success, *Doonesbury* was also growing up.

Doonesbury Expands

In 1971 Trudeau entered Yale's graduate school, concentrating on graphic arts to improve his artistic skills in case the initial success of *Doonesbury* did not last. As he had feared while an undergraduate, combining classwork and a daily comic strip stretched him to the limit. To help lighten his workload, Trudeau hired a freelance artist named Don Carlton to ink his penciled strips, the kind of arrangement used by many cartoonists.

> "Cartoonists do concern themselves with the truth, but if they delivered it straight, they would totally fail in their roles as humorists."[32]
>
> —*Garry Trudeau*

As *Doonesbury* was picked up by more newspapers, Trudeau began changing from college-oriented humor toward more general topics and sharpening his liberal pen. Trudeau's detractors often question his use of satire against the public figures he covers, characterizing it as unfair. Trudeau answers these critics:

> What is lacking in such a question is a fundamental understanding of the nature of comedy. . . . Cartoonists do concern themselves with the truth, but if they delivered it straight, they would totally fail in their roles as humorists. Therefore, I feel no obligation to be "fair" in any absolute sense to a subject simply because certain individuals are sensitive to it.[32]

In the 1970s there was no shortage of individuals, especially politicians, for *Doonesbury* to ridicule. Unlike other cartoonists, who gave pseudonyms to the real-life people in their strips, Trudeau boldly used his subjects' real names. Presidents and other politicians were often drawn as a symbol that depicted Trudeau's interpretation of the person's character. For example, in later decades, he drew President Bill Clinton as a waffle, to symbolize the idea that Clinton "waffled," or changed his mind often, on important issues.

One of the biggest news stories of the 1970s, however, was the Watergate scandal, which revealed the Nixon administration's involvement in the cover-up of a burglary of the headquarters of the Democratic National Committee in Washington, DC's, Watergate Hotel. Trudeau chronicled the fates of the Republicans accused of involvement in the cover-up. One Watergate strip pronounced Attorney General John Mitchell, an alleged co-conspirator, guilty before his trial. Outraged editors of the *Washington Post* canceled the strip and wrote to Universal Press, "If anyone is going to find any defendant guilty, it's going to be the due process of justice, not a comic strip artist."[33] Trudeau later commented that he was not really saying Mitchell was guilty but simply satirizing the overheated media rhetoric that surrounded the Watergate scandal.

In 1975, Trudeau won a Pulitzer Prize for *Doonesbury*. It was the first time a comic strip, rather than a single-panel editorial cartoon, had captured the prestigious award. By the 1980s *Doonesbury* had become an established satirical commentary, with an audience of more than 18 million readers. But for Trudeau the new decade also meant some changes.

Marriage and Time Off

In June 1980 Trudeau married Jane Pauley, a cohost on the NBC morning show, *Today*. After a simple outdoor ceremony, the newlyweds delayed their honeymoon trip to Paris by a day so that Trudeau, always diligent about his work, could meet a *Doonesbury* deadline. The couple has experienced trying times, including two miscarriages and Pauley's diagnosis of bipolar disorder. They have three children and careers that have put them both at one time or another in the public eye. Trudeau is well-known

Gary Trudeau and wife, Jane Pauley, attend the Time 100 Gala in 2013. The couple married in 1980 and have three children. Pauley, a television journalist, still works as a correspondent and guest host on CBS news shows.

for his reluctance to be interviewed in the media. His explanation for shunning the spotlight is simple: "Everything I have to share I share in the strip."[34]

In 1982, Trudeau made cartoon history: he announced that he would be taking an extended leave of absence from drawing *Doonesbury* beginning in January 1983. Such an action was unheard of in an industry where cartoonists are under contract to their syndicates, but Trudeau nevertheless decided that he needed time to refresh himself and the strip. Reprints of old strips filled in *Doonesbury*'s space in the newspapers until Trudeau's return. Although he was only thirty-four years old, he explained that "investigative cartooning is a young man's game."[35] Trudeau's announcement distressed *Doonesbury* fans, but he was not idle during his leave. Collaborating with theatrical composer Elizabeth Swados, Trudeau created *Doonesbury*, a Broadway musical based on the strip. It ran for 104 performances in 1983 and 1984, garnering several award nominations but mixed reviews.

In Trudeau's musical, the gang finally graduates from Walden College. When Trudeau returned to writing his daily and Sunday strips, the newspaper incarnation of Mike Doonesbury and friends also experienced a transformation.

Life After Walden

For more than ten years, Mike, B.D., and the others were perpetual college students who never aged. After his leave, Trudeau allowed his characters to grow older and have real-life experiences, both good and bad. Mike married twice and had a daughter named Alex. Andy Lippincott, a gay character afflicted with AIDS, succumbed to the disease. When B.D. lost his leg in Iraq, reader reaction to the story was touching. "I was talking to a soldier in the hospital," Trudeau recalls, "and I said, 'I draw this comic strip, and I have this character named B.D. who lost his leg.' The soldier's eyes widened: 'B.D. lost his leg?!' Here's this mangled, broken hero lying in his bed, and he's concerned that this character he knows had such a terrible thing happen to him. It was very moving."[36] Trudeau donated the proceeds of a book featuring the strips telling B.D.'s story to Fisher House Foundation, a nonprofit organization helping military families.

> "I was talking to a soldier in the hospital. . . . Here's this mangled, broken hero lying in his bed, and he's concerned that this character he knows [B.D.] had such a terrible thing happen to him. It was very moving."[36]
>
> —*Garry Trudeau*

Trudeau Visits the Troops

Before writing the series of strips dealing with B.D.'s wounding and rehabilitation, Trudeau visited injured soldiers to learn about their real-life experiences. This excerpt of a Trudeau speech is from the *San Francisco Chronicle* website.

I recently spent the day in Silver Spring, Md., at a Veterans of Foreign Wars post and a vet center, talking to two veterans of Operation Enduring Freedom who are about to leave the service and make their way back into civilian life. Both have grievous wounds. One is an amputee, the other has metal plates in his back and a head full of brutal memories. . . .

Both soldiers, with the help of incredibly dedicated counselors, are trying to figure out how to live with their emotional wounds as they make the transition out of a military culture that still stigmatizes post-traumatic stress syndrome, and then into a civilian population that can't possibly understand what they've been through.

The reason that I've been listening to their stories is that my character B.D. is now at that precise point in his own life, and I need to learn about what that must feel like before I can write about it. When and if I finally do, I have to do another terrible thing: I have to make it funny. And I have to find a way of doing so without contributing to the suffering that these young veterans are enduring.

Garry Trudeau, "Behind the Lines: *Doonesbury* Cartoonist Pulls Duty Getting to Know Soldiers and Their Problems to Make Strip Authentic," SFGate, October 23, 2005. www.sfgate.com.

Through *Doonesbury*, Trudeau has dealt with such topics as AIDS, abortion, the tobacco industry, the National Rifle Association, and same-sex marriage. These controversial subjects have prompted many newspapers to move *Doonesbury* from the comics page to the editorial section. It has also become common for papers to drop the strip when it deals with a topic that the editors feel would alienate their readers. Trudeau has lampooned presidents from Nixon to Clinton, especially George H.W. Bush and Clinton's successor, George W. Bush. So critical was Trudeau toward the Bushes that many conservatives charged that he was waging a personal vendetta against them, to which Trudeau states, "Of course not. It's never personal."[37]

The January 2015 murder of eleven people at the French satirical newspaper *Charlie Hebdo* embroiled Trudeau in his own controversy. The killings, perpetrated by two radical Islamists, were prompted by the paper's publishing of cartoons depicting the prophet Muhammad, which is considered blasphemy by followers of the Islamic faith. In a speech three months later, Trudeau commented on the tragedy, saying that "by attacking a powerless, disenfranchised minority with crude, vulgar drawings closer to graffiti than cartoons, *Charlie* wandered into the realm of hate speech."[38] Trudeau was roundly criticized for his apparent attempt to lay blame on the victims. He later clarified his position, saying that he "should have made it a little clearer that I was as outraged as the rest of the world at the time. I mourn them deeply."[39]

> "When people tell me they keep up with the news through *Doonesbury*, I tremble for the republic, but the truth is, everyone has time for the comics."[40]
>
> —*Garry Trudeau*

In an age of social media and declining newspaper readership, Trudeau is confident about the future of his chosen art form. "If comics were important in a pre-literate America," he comments, "they are absolutely indispensable is a post-literate one. When people tell me they keep up with the news through *Doonesbury*, I tremble for the republic, but the truth is, everyone has time for the comics."[40] As his success has proved, a lot of people have time to view the world through the eyes of Trudeau's *Doonesbury*.

CHAPTER 3

Lynn Johnston

C omic strips are full of amazing and amusing characters. From the denizens of *Sherman's Lagoon* to the inhabitants of the future world of *Brewster Rockit: Space Guy*, these characters live in fantasy worlds where anything can—and usually does—happen. But some cartoonists forsake the imaginary and instead draw strips that examine everyday life. To see reality reflected in the characters of a comic strip can elicit an enjoyable sense of familiarity from its readers, who may think, "Wow, I can relate to that!"

One of the most popular and enduring of these strips is *For Better or For Worse* by Canadian cartoonist Lynn Johnston. Using the experiences of her own life, Johnston created a comic strip family that has become as real to millions of readers as their own families. It takes courage to put one's own successes and failures into print for all to see, but Johnston has displayed such courage by allowing the fictional family in *For Better or For Worse* to cope with both the joys and sorrows of life.

An Artistic Upbringing

Lynn Ridgeway Johnston was destined almost from birth to be an artist. She was born on May 28, 1947, to parents Mervyn and

Ursula Ridgeway in Collingwood, Ontario. Lynn inherited her artistic talent from her mother, who was skilled in various media, including painting, sculpting, and calligraphy. From her father, she acquired an interest in comedy and comics from his vast collection of cartoon books. Lynn was also influenced by her aunt, Unity Bainbridge, also a talented artist. "There was no question about it," she recalls. "I was going to be an artist like Aunt Unity. Everyone said so and I knew it was true. I had been able to draw since the age of two."[41]

In 1949 the Ridgeway family moved to North Vancouver, British Columbia. In a home without television, Lynn made funny drawings to entertain her younger brother, Alan, who roared with appreciative laughter. But not everything was funny in Lynn's young life. Her mother's inability to compliment her children led Lynn to have rather low self-esteem. She recalls, "My mother never praised us. . . . I grew up thinking that nothing I did was good enough and that I wasn't good enough either."[42] In elementary school, Lynn acted out, often using her artistic talent to make unflattering drawings of her teachers. She was no stranger to the principal's office, yet she would also come to the aid of any friend in need, solving problems with her fists if necessary.

In high school, Lynn continued to caricature teachers, but she also created illustrations for the school yearbook, eventually becoming its editor. This responsibility built up her confidence as an artist. She explains, "I began to see myself as a graphic artist who could take on a complex project—and make it happen."[43] After graduating in 1965, Lynn enrolled in the Vancouver School of Art, a fine arts college. Her time there confirmed that her strengths and interests lay not in painting or sculpting but in commercial illustration. With her talent and sense of humor, a career in cartooning was not far off.

> "I was going to be an artist like Aunt Unity. Everyone said so and I knew it was true. I had been able to draw since the age of two."[41]
>
> —Lynn Johnston

Becoming a Professional

On a summer break from art school, Lynn worked at an animation studio, inking and painting the acetate cels that the characters

Canadian cartoonist Lynn Johnston is known for her syndicated strip For Better or For Worse. As the title suggests, the characters in her family-centered strip experience the highs and lows of life, making them believable and beloved by readers.

are drawn on. Through a friend at her job she met Doug Franks, a television cameraman, whom she married in 1967. The couple soon moved to Hamilton, Ontario, where Lynn found work as a graphic artist at McMaster University Medical Centre, a teaching hospital. For five years she drew medical illustrations and applied her talent for cartooning to creating humorous graphics for medical lectures. In her free time she produced illustrations for a growing number of freelance clients.

While her art career was blossoming, her personal life was in turmoil. Lynn wanted to have children, but Doug did not. "The subject of baby drove a wedge between us,"[44] she explains. Soon, however, she learned that she was pregnant, and their marriage seemed to improve. Aware of her artistic talent, Dr. Murray Enkin, her obstetrician, asked Lynn to draw some cartoons to entertain his patients. She created a series of eighty cartoons depicting the ups and downs of pregnancy for the doctor's examination room.

On April 11, 1973, the Franks' first child, Aaron, was born. But Lynn's joy at motherhood was short-lived: her troubled marriage finally collapsed, and she and Doug divorced. Lynn struggled with the stress of being a single mother along with keeping her freelance art business going. Then one day, Dr. Enkin invited her to dinner. "Murray sat on the floor," Lynn remembers, "with all

Mtigwaki

When Lynn and her husband lived in the tiny northern Canadian town of Lynn Lake, they met many people of the First Nations, a term that has replaced *Indians* in describing aboriginal Canadians. Twenty years later, Johnston sought to incorporate the uniqueness of the culture and its friendly people into *For Better or For Worse*.

I wanted to create an imaginary Ojibway community in Northern Ontario that would be true to life, giving readers a realistic view of what living in a First Nation community is like. In so doing, I wanted to show Elizabeth's world change for the better, with the challenge of teaching multiple grades in an unfamiliar environment, rich with Canadian history.

With the help of some First Nations friends, Johnston created the fictional community of Mtigwaki, a name that means "Land of Trees." In a series of strips in 2004, Elizabeth, who has become a teacher, goes north to teach the children of Mtigwaki. She learns Ojibway words and experiences native ceremonies, such as a powwow complete with native dancing. Although she enjoys teaching the children, homesickness eventually gets the best of her and she returns home.

Johnston was awarded the 2004 Debwewin Citation, an award for excellence in journalism about the aboriginal peoples of Canada. *Debwewin* is the Ojibway word for "truth," and Johnston received the honor for her portrayal of First Nations citizens not as stereotypes but as real people.

Lynn Johnston, "Mtigwaki (Land of Trees)," *For Better or For Worse*. www.fborfw.com.

eighty cartoons I had drawn . . . spread around him like a great fan. 'Kid,' he said as he popped the cork on a champagne bottle, 'you've got a book.'"[45]

Getting Published

With Dr. Enkin's help Lynn found a publisher, and her first book of cartoons, entitled *David, We're Pregnant!*, was published in 1974. Two more books followed, *Hi, Mom! Hi Dad!* and *Do They Ever Grow Up?*, chronicling the joys and trials of raising children. Also following her first book was her marriage to Rod Johnston, a dental student with ambitions of bringing free dental services to remote Canadian locations via private airplane.

In 1977, while Rod was finishing dental school, Lynn received a call from Universal Press Syndicate. James Andrews, a partner in the company, had seen her books and was looking for a new strip to syndicate. Johnston sent twenty sample strips about a family and waited for a response. "When we saw Lynn's work we loved it," remarks Lee Salem, who at the time was editor at Universal Press. "What attracted us was the mother's perspective and the somewhat wry tone she would take on her situation and her husband's life and children's lives."[46] Johnston signed a twenty-year contract with Universal Press for a daily and Sunday comic strip. "I was brand new at this and scared to death," she remembers. "On the other hand, this was the biggest door that had ever been opened for me! All I could do was my best."[47]

> "What attracted us [to Lynn's work] was the mother's perspective and the somewhat wry tone she would take on her situation and her husband's life and children's lives."[46]
>
> —Lee Salem, editor, Universal Press Syndicate.

Between signing the contract in 1978 and the strip's debut, Johnston concentrated on improving her humor. "I wanted to practice writing dialogue, learn timing and technique,"[48] she recalls. Salem suggested calling the strip *For Better or For Worse*, because that was, in a nutshell, what it would be about. The family became the Pattersons, and Johnston used her family members' middle names for most of her cartoon family. Rod became John, the father who, like his namesake, was a dentist. The children were Michael (from Aaron), and Elizabeth (from daughter Kate, born in 1977). For the all-important homemaker and mother character, Johnston chose not her own middle name, but Elly, as a tribute to a friend who had died as a child. Even so, Elly Patterson was definitely Lynn Johnston in personality and temperament.

Life with the Pattersons

Johnston got her ideas for *For Better or For Worse* from her own experiences, which now centered around life in the remote town of Lynn Lake in northern Manitoba. The Johnstons had moved there when Rod graduated from dental school and established his flying dental practice. Johnston's neighbors and acquaintances in Lynn Lake provided fodder for the strip. "I've always based characters on real people," she says, "and the stories are part truth, part fiction. I like to research the material so that situations, if not true, are at least believable."[49]

> "I've always based characters on real people, and the stories are part truth, part fiction. I like to research the material so that situations, if not true, are at least believable."[49]
>
> —Lynn Johnston

For Better or For Worse began its syndicated run on September 9, 1979. Elly, John, and the children had adventures that most young parents could identify with: active children getting into mischief, frazzled parents doing their best at parenting, and late night reflections on the changes that kids bring to a relationship. Johnston created the strip in her home studio, first penciling the strips and then inking them and adding shading as necessary. Working in the mornings and after the children were in bed, she could draw and ink a week of strips in two days, sending them to Universal Press in Kansas City, Missouri, by courier. The rest of Johnston's time was spent with community activities, raising children, and trying to maintain a contented household. In 1985, Johnston became the first woman cartoonist (and first Canadian) to win the prestigious Reuben Award from the National Cartoonists Society.

The Pattersons welcomed another daughter, April, to the family in a strip in 1991. *For Better or For Worse* also began expanding with new characters and situations, some of which brought the family-oriented strip into new and controversial territory.

Drawing from Life

For Better or For Worse was based on gentle humor, but for Johnston, there were also serious issues to address. One character who had to work through a difficult issue was Michael's friend Lawrence. After years of feeling "different," Lawrence confided to Michael that he was gay. "It felt right for Lawrence to be gay," Johnston comments. "He was like so many people I know who have had to deal with this traumatic realization and who have

Realification

If the world of the Pattersons seems real, it is because Johnston takes great pains to make it so. She explains her methods for creating realism in her book *For Better or Worse: The Art of Lynn Johnston.*

I also drew an aerial view of the neighbourhood and the town where the Pattersons lived. This was extremely helpful in that it gave me a clear view of my own imaginary comic strip world. It was also the beginning of the "realification" of everything. . . . From then on, everything I drew came from something I saw, experienced, felt, or knew to be true. I tried to make things look like things. I used toys, for example, to give me perspective on everything from cars to fridges to Rollerblades. One of the most useful toys I have is a small wire shopping cart. Try drawing a shopping cart from memory! I have toy animals, toy hats, and sports equipment. If there was a toy out there I could use to draw from, I bought it. Another great find was a miniature drum set, which I featured in April's band. I had an "*ah-hah* moment" when I discovered that toys made great drawing tools. This is one of the tricks of the trade that I enjoy sharing with young artists.

Lynn Johnston and Katherine Hadway, *For Better or For Worse: The Comic Art of Lynn Johnston.* Fredericton, New Brunswick, Canada: Goose Lane, 2015, pp. 137–38.

done so with courage and honesty."[50] Lawrence's revelation and its consequences played out in a four-week series of strips.

Even before the series began, forty newspapers declined to run it and requested alternate strips. Within a week of its start, nineteen papers permanently canceled *For Better or For Worse*. Angry letters flooded newspapers that ran the series; Johnston herself received thousands of letters, some positive, others containing unnerving verbal abuse. It was the first time that *For Better or For Worse* had gotten such angry criticism, and Johnston lost a good deal of sleep over the reaction. But it was an invaluable lesson. "I learned that the comics page is a powerful communicator," she recalls. "Those of us who produce these panels have a responsibility to . . . our audience to use this space with conscience and with care. I believe I did that with this story. I believe it made a difference."[51]

Another strip that generated considerable reader reaction was when Farley, the Patterson's lovable sheepdog, died after rescuing April from a raging river. Farley was one of the most popular characters in *For Better or For Worse*, and his death shocked and saddened readers. But Farley lives on in name and likeness, donated by Johnston to the Farley Foundation, which provides financial assistance to low-income pet owners. Other strips dealt with such topics as Elizabeth's being assaulted by a coworker; Elly's elderly father, Jim, suffering a stroke and subsequently losing speech; and the experiences of a teenage character with intellectual disabilities.

By 1994, *For Better or For Worse* was appearing in sixteen hundred newspapers, and books featuring collections of the strips were selling briskly. Johnston's readership was growing, and so was her business.

Expanding and Growing Up

Johnston realized that she needed help for her expanding workload, which she describes: "I did artwork for various non-profit groups around town, we did a series of little books, made calendars and greeting cards, and cover art for the collection books."[52] There was even a series of animated television shows featuring the Pattersons. Soon her team included a graphic designer, a business manager, and a web developer. Johnston's husband

Balancing her art, her public appearances, and other work was difficult for Lynn Johnston (shown here at the 2005 New York Book Expo), so when her strip became more popular, she enlisted the aid of a business manager and even her own husband to help out with daily tasks.

cut back on his dental practice to help out. While the business side of *For Better or For* Worse matured, so did the lives of the Patterson family.

Unlike the characters in many comic strips, the Pattersons grew older in real time. Michael eventually got married, as did

Elizabeth, and April became a veterinarian. John and Elly's future included travel, raising grandchildren, and doing volunteer work together. But the happy outcome of their life did not match the reality of Lynn and Rod Johnston's relationship. In 2007, the Johnstons separated and ultimately divorced. The end of *For Better or For Worse* came a year later when, on August 31, 2008, the final strip was published. In it, Johnston appears in the last panel, thanking her syndicate, her family, and her readers for twenty-nine years of devotion to her work. Although the first run of *For Better or For Worse* and her marriage were over, Johnston was making plans for the future.

Life Without Deadlines

In her final strip, Johnston wrote, "Please join me on Monday as the story begins again . . . with new insights and new smiles. Looking back looks wonderful."[53] The day after the original *For Better or For Worse* ended, it began running again from the beginning, giving a new generation of readers a chance to share the Pattersons' lives. The reruns initially mixed old, new, and reworked strips, but beginning in 2010, only old strips were printed, with minor changes to update older references. The strip appears today in newspapers and on the *For Better or For Worse* website.

As a retired cartoonist, Johnston continues to stretch her artistic muscles in new directions. After drawing whimsical cartoons on a dress she planned to wear at an awards ceremony, the idea of bringing her talent to fabric art began to take hold. A line of neckties featuring fanciful animals, fish, and cartoon words in Johnston's inimitable style is offered for sale on her website. *For Better or For Worse* calendars and books are still popular items with Johnston's fans. She still creates illustrations for articles and books, as well as drawing occasional pictures for the Farley Foundation. Her staff is busy cataloging and archiving the massive amount of original art Johnston has generated throughout her more than thirty-year career.

Even in retirement Johnston says, "I am still a cartoonist, and even if some folks don't call it fine art, it's fine with me. I have had the best life ever!"[54] Her loyal readers are delighted that she has shared that life with them.

CHAPTER 4

Seth MacFarlane

For more than fifty years, the citizens of the small town of Kent, Connecticut, have gotten news and entertainment from their weekly newspaper, *The Kent Good Times Dispatch*. In the 1980s, a comic strip called *Walter Crouton* appeared in the *Dispatch*, drawn by a local artist. One week, when readers opened up their paper, they saw that the artist had drawn an irreverent cartoon in which Walter, kneeling at an altar to receive Communion, asks, "Can I have fries with that?"[55] A local priest was outraged by the sacrilegious humor and sent an angry letter to the artist, an eleven-year-old boy named Seth MacFarlane. MacFarlane later said that the cartoon created a "mini controversy"[56] in the small community. It was a foretaste of the kind of humor that would make him a multimillionaire as the creator of *Family Guy* and other animated television series.

Young Cartoonist

Seth Woodbury MacFarlane was born on October 26, 1973, in Kent, Connecticut. His father, Ronald, was a butcher turned history teacher, and his mother, Perry, worked in the administration office of Kent School, a private prep school. His only sibling, sister Rachael, was born in 1976. Ronald recalls that Seth was "a little apart from everyone else. There's a side of him that I can't quite get to. He never really liked being hugged or touched."[57]

MacFarlane began drawing around the age of two, sitting in front of the family TV and sketching cartoon characters from *The Flintstones* television show. Animation fascinated him and stimulated his curious mind. "When I was old enough to ask the question," MacFarlane recalls, "I was asking, 'How are cartoons made? How do I do one of these?'"[58] His parents encouraged his interest in creating animated cartoons. "I knew by five that I wanted to get into animation," he remembers. "And I think my parents found one book on animation, that they scrounged up for me, and they got it from a library, you know, two towns over."[59]

At the age of nine, MacFarlane got his first paying job drawing cartoons for Kent's newspaper, the *Kent Good Times Dispatch*. His comic strip, *Walter Crouton*, appeared weekly, and he was paid five dollars for each installment. MacFarlane's humor in *Walter Crouton* was not always as controversial as his communion panel, relying rather on typical cartoon gags. For example, one strip shows Walter as a baseball player calling, "I got it! I got it!" as he runs to catch a pop fly, only to be crushed by a huge baseball landing on him.

Breaking Into Animation

MacFarlane attended high school at Kent School, continuing to practice his drawing there, as well as trying his hand at animation with an 8mm camera his parents had given him. After graduating in 1991, he enrolled at the Rhode Island School of Design (RISD), considered one of the best art schools in the nation. MacFarlane

> "[Seth was] a little apart from everyone else. There's a side of him that I can't quite get to. He never really liked being hugged or touched."[57]
>
> —Ronald MacFarlane, Seth's father.

Seth MacFarlane checks over storyboard art for his 2012 film Ted. *The movie, which starred an obnoxious and foul-mouthed teddy bear, exemplifies the type of crass humor that has come to characterize MacFarlane's television shows and big-screen productions.*

studied film and animation, creating student films with an eye toward working at Walt Disney Studios after graduation. During his college years, MacFarlane became interested in a television series called *The Simpsons*, a half-hour animated comedy created by cartoonist Matt Groening. MacFarlane recalls his reaction to Groening's creation.

> His show redirected the course of where I wanted my life to go. I wanted to be a Disney animator and then *The Simpsons* came out, and in every way—writing-wise, production-wise, timing-wise, animation-wise—it just rewrote the rulebook. Suddenly I was laughing out loud at cartoons. . . . I remember thinking, "Oh my God, this is what I want to do."[60]

The Simpsons's simple animation and offbeat comedy style sparked MacFarlane's creativity, which he applied to his student films. His instructors did not know quite what to make of MacFarlane's unique brand of humor. "My professors were caught between being unbelievably supportive and invaluable in the education that they gave me and being completely horrified by the type of work I was doing,"[61] he says. That work would lead MacFarlane to create his own animated cartoon series.

Before *Family Guy*

As his senior thesis, MacFarlane made a ten-minute animated film called *The Life of Larry*. He not only produced, wrote, and directed the film, but did most of the voices and drew the animation frame by frame, a process that took months to complete. *The Life of Larry* captivated the college audience when he screened it at RISD. Two of his instructors were so impressed that they entered the film in a competition sponsored by the Hanna-Barbera animation studio, the company that produced *The Flintstones* and other popular TV cartoons. *The Life of Larry* won the competition, and as a result, MacFarlane was

"*[The Simpsons]* rewrote the rulebook. Suddenly I was laughing out loud at cartoons. . . . I remember thinking, 'Oh my God, this is what I want to do.'"[60]

—Seth MacFarlane

MacFarlane's Musical Talents

Seth McFarlane is a man of many voices on his television shows *Family Guy* and *American Dad!*, but his vocal talent goes beyond the animated characters he brings to life. As a child, MacFarlane listened to Broadway and movie musicals and records of the Big Band era of the 1930s and 1940s. That eventually encouraged him to use his smooth baritone voice to sing the songs he grew up with. His taste in music is decidedly old school, and he counts singers from past decades such as Dean Martin and Bing Crosby among his musical inspirations. The most significant influence on his singing style is Frank Sinatra; MacFarlane even took voice lessons from Sinatra's vocal coach.

In 2011, MacFarlane released his first album, entitled *Music Is Better than Words*. The album is filled with vintage songs and is, according to MacFarlane, a classic Sinatra-style album. He even used one of Sinatra's old microphones in the recording sessions. Despite mixed reviews, *Music Is Better than Words* was nominated for a Grammy Award. MacFarlane released two other albums, *Holiday for Swing* and *No One Ever Tells You*, the latter earning a Grammy nomination in 2016.

If anyone doubts that MacFarlane is serious about music, they need only listen to an episode of *Family Guy* or *American Dad!* Although most other animated shows use electronic music to save money, MacFarlane's shows employ a full forty-five-piece orchestra.

offered a job at the studio. Just twenty-two years old, MacFarlane packed his bags and headed for Hollywood.

At Hanna-Barbera, MacFarlane wrote scripts and created storyboards for the animated shows *Dexter's Lab*, *Cow and Chicken*, and *Johnny Bravo*. "I spent the most time on *Johnny Bravo*," MacFarlane recalls, "and as a series, the comedic style, it was sort of freer than anywhere else to sort of write with my own style."[62] While at Hanna-Barbera, he created a sequel to *The Life of Larry* called *Larry and Steve*. His two *Larry* films caught the eye of executives at the Fox Broadcasting Company, who wanted to meet him and learn more about his ambitions.

Creating *Family Guy*

With script and character sketches in hand, MacFarlane met with Fox executives but without success. A year later, however, as MacFarlane explains, "they said, 'If you can do [a pilot] for $50,000, we'll give you a shot at a series.'"[63] He says, "I spent about six months with no sleep and no life, just drawing like crazy in my kitchen and doing this pilot."[64] His exhausting work paid off: Fox ordered thirteen episodes of *Family Guy*, making MacFarlane the youngest executive producer to win a prime-time television slot.

MacFarlane describes *Family Guy* as a show "about a fictional Rhode Island family that uses the animation medium to satirize everything from pop culture to politics, and is really out to make you laugh."[65] The show's family, the Griffins, includes the dull-witted father, Peter; his wife, Lois; and their three children: teenagers Meg and Chris and Stewie, a diabolical one-year-old who speaks with a British accent and is obsessed with killing his mother. Rounding out the cast is Brian, the talking dog who loves martinis and is the smartest one in the family. MacFarlane provides the voices of Peter, Stewie, and Brian, as well as other characters on the show. One of the hallmarks of the show is the use of cutaway gags, short comedy bits that have little or no bearing on the main plot.

> "I spent about six months with no sleep and no life, just drawing like crazy in my kitchen and doing [the *Family Guy*] pilot."[64]
>
> —Seth MacFarlane

MacFarlane gives the show its edgy, often crude brand of humor, a trait that runs in his family. Says MacFarlane's sister, Rachael, "I think my brother and I both get our senses of humor from our parents. I mean, my mother was absolutely hilarious and foul. She had the most ridiculously off color sense of humor, so that was sort of what we grew up with."[66]

On the Air

Family Guy debuted on Sunday, January 31, 1999, following the broadcast of Super Bowl XXXIII. Twenty-two million viewers saw the first episode, which garnered generally good reviews. In 2000 MacFarlane won an Emmy Award for his voicing of Stewie. But Fox changed the show's time slot several times, and *Family Guy*'s audience steadily declined. In 2002 the network canceled the show due to low ratings. Reruns of *Family Guy* began airing on Cartoon Network's *Adult Swim*, however, whose late-night lineup of animated programs appealed to a young male audience. Ratings improved, and Fox ultimately brought *Family Guy* back to its schedule, the first such comeback in broadcast history.

Family Guy became a staple of the Fox network's roster of animated shows, beginning its fourteenth season in September 2015. Millions of viewers have tuned in to enjoy the antics of the Griffin clan as well as to see just how far the show would push the bounds of decency. But not everyone is a fan of MacFarlane's brand of humor.

Since its first airing in 1999, Family Guy *has courted controversy for its jokes about religion, politics, sex, and other sensitive subjects. Teenage and young adult audiences, though, tend to be drawn to its crude humor and the fact that nothing is held too sacred to satirize.*

The Critics Speak

Criticism of *Family Guy* has centered on the show's rough language, sexual themes, and stories that satirize such sensitive topics as rape, religion, people with special needs, and domestic violence. Some critics complained that *Family Guy* was a blatant rip-off of *The Simpsons*, while others condemned the crude humor that made the show a hit with young audiences. The headmaster of MacFarlane's alma mater, the Kent School, called for a

Exploring the Cosmos

For thirteen weeks in 1980, the Public Broadcasting Service's science program *Cosmos: A Personal Voyage* brought the wonders of space and humanity's place in the universe to more than 700 million viewers. With personable astronomer Carl Sagan presenting difficult concepts in understandable terms, the show changed the way people looked at science.

Fast forward to the twenty-first century and a new generation that could benefit from a fresh look at the wonders of science. MacFarlane, a lifelong fan of Sagan's work, became executive producer of a revamped incarnation of Sagan's show called *Cosmos: A Spacetime Odyssey*. Astrophysicist Neil deGrasse Tyson, director of the Hayden Planetarium in New York City, took over the host role that Sagan originated.

In 2008, MacFarlane met Tyson, who later introduced him to Ann Druyan (Sagan's widow), and producers Brannon Braga and Mitchell Cannold, who were interested in resurrecting *Cosmos.* After several years of planning, MacFarlane proposed the show to the Fox Network, and a deal was made for thirteen episodes. The program aired in the spring of 2014 on Fox and the National Geographic Channel, as well as in more than 180 countries around the world. It won four Primetime Emmy Awards, a Peabody Award (which recognizes outstanding public service in the media), and numerous other accolades. Among the new elements of the series were animated segments about "great people who, in some cases suffered the ultimate sacrifice in order to get new knowledge," says Druyan. "That's a result of Seth MacFarlane's involvement."

Quoted in Susan Karlin, "A Science Odyssey: How the Makers of 'Cosmos' Reinvented a Classic," *Fast Company.* www.fastcocreate.com.

boycott of the program. The Parents Television Council, a group advocating family-appropriate television, said *Family Guy* "delivers some of the most vile, offensive content on broadcast television. . . . Language is a major issue, with bleeped expletives . . . used frequently."[67] Even other cartoonists criticized *Family Guy*. John Kricfalusi, creator of the cartoon *Ren and Stimpy*, disparaged *Family Guy's* simple animation style, saying, "You can draw Family Guy when you're ten years old. . . . The standards are extremely low."[68] Trey Parker and Matt Stone, creators of *South Park*, criticized *Family Guy's* writing and use of cutaway gags.

> "The *Family Guy* crowd and the *Simpsons* crowd have become friendly over time. I thought the *South Park* episode making fun of us was funny and accurate."[69]
>
> —Seth MacFarlane

MacFarlane takes the criticism in stride. "The *Family Guy* crowd and the *Simpsons* crowd have become friendly over time," he states. "I thought the *South Park* episode making fun of us was funny and accurate."[69] After fourteen seasons of *Family Guy*, the critics may be mellowing. At the Critics' Choice Television Awards ceremony on May 31, 2015, MacFarlane received the Louis XIII Genius Award. He accepted the honor with his usual humor, saying, "The word [genius] gets thrown around a lot, which is good because otherwise I probably wouldn't be getting this."[70]

MacFarlane does not need a trophy to be recognized as a genius, however. His successes in many areas of show business are evidence of his intellect and varied talents.

New Animated Families

When *Family Guy* was canceled in 2002, MacFarlane was already working on another animated show. *American Dad!* tells the story of Stan Smith, a super-patriotic but dull-witted CIA agent, and his family, which looks somewhat like the Griffins of *Family Guy*. Stan has a wife; a son and daughter (the latter voiced by Rachael MacFarlane); Klaus, a talking German goldfish; and an alien named Roger. MacFarlane does the voices of Stan and Roger, and designed the characters that are brought to life by some fifty animators. *American Dad!* began its eleventh season in January 2016, with an order for two more seasons to be broadcast through 2018.

While *Family Guy* and *American Dad!* featured predominantly white characters, MacFarlane's next animated series starred an African American family. MacFarlane created *The Cleveland Show*, featuring Cleveland Brown, a character appearing in *Family Guy*, and his dysfunctional family. Debuting on Fox in 2009, *The Cleveland Show* was similar to MacFarlane's other animated shows, but with an increase in racial humor. Initially popular with audiences, its ratings steadily declined, and in 2013 it was canceled.

From Small to Big Screen

After his success with animation on television, MacFarlane turned to live-action films. In 2012 he wrote and directed the comedy *Ted*, his first theatrical film. The title character is a teddy bear who has come to life and lives with his adult owner. Voiced by MacFarlane, the computer-animated bear's vulgar language and crude humor earned the film an R rating but also huge numbers at the box office, where it grossed more than $500 million worldwide. The film's theme song, cowritten by MacFarlane, was nominated for an Academy Award for best original song.

MacFarlane starred in his next film, 2014's *A Million Ways to Die in the West*. Despite a cast that included such major stars as Liam Neeson and Charlize Theron, the western comedy was a disappointment at the box office. Audiences were also indifferent to MacFarlane's third live-action movie, a sequel entitled *Ted 2*. Released in 2015, it received mixed reviews and an underwhelming box office performance.

Although MacFarlane's films may not be the kind that win Academy Awards, in 2013 he hosted the Eighty-Fifth Academy Awards ceremony. MacFarlane's performance featured his edgy humor, opening with a risqué song-and-dance number, followed by jibes at celebrities in the audience, some of whom were less than pleased at his comments. When asked on Twitter if he might host future award shows, MacFarlane commented, "No way. Lotta fun to have done it though."[71]

If presenting awards is not in MacFarlane's future, receiving them just may be. At Comic-Con 2015, MacFarlane said a new live-action comedy show was "not out of the question."[72] New episodes of *Family Guy* and *American Dad!* are in production, and *Bordertown*, an animated sitcom with MacFarlane as executive producer, debuted on Fox in January 2016.

MacFarlane is content in his personal life as an eligible bachelor with a history of dating Hollywood actresses. He contributes to various causes, including giving $1 million in 2014 to Reading Rainbow's Kickstarter campaign for children's literacy, as well as donating to various civic projects in his home town of Kent, Connecticut, and to the Democratic Party. An atheist who was named Harvard Humanist of the Year in 2011, MacFarlane is also a staunch advocate of gay rights.

No matter what creative projects he decides to take on in the coming years, MacFarlane's fans can be sure that he will continue to push boundaries and poke fun at social conventions. But above all, he will continue to make people laugh.

CHAPTER 5

Matt Groening

S pringfield is one of the most common geographical place names in the United States; the US Postal Service identifies forty-one locations that bear the name. But there is one Springfield that cannot be found on any map, although it may be the most famous of them all. It is the town where Homer Simpson and his family reside in the animated sitcom world of *The Simpsons*. Created by cartoonist Matt Groening, *The Simpsons* is the longest-running scripted television series of all time and the winner of more than thirty Primetime Emmy Awards, television's highest honor. *Time* magazine called it the best TV show of the 20th century. It is an impressive achievement for Groening, whose father once pointedly told him, "You can't draw."[73]

Early Years

Matthew Abram Groening (rhymes with "raining") was born in Portland, Oregon, on February 15, 1954. The Groening family consisted of Matt's father, Homer, a filmmaker and cartoonist; mother Margaret, a former teacher; and his four siblings, Mark, Patty, Lisa, and Maggie. Despite growing up in a devoutly Methodist home, Matt was ambivalent about religion, leading him to characterize himself as an agnostic later in life. The Groening home was near the Portland Zoo, where Matt often played. He says, "I used to sneak on the zoo train for free rides, and when they moved the zoo to a new location my friends and I would play in the old bear grotto and go swimming in the bear pool."[74] Matt was not fond of school, once comparing it to a World War II prisoner of war camp. His disruptive nature often got him into trouble, and on more than one occasion he could be found in the principal's office or writing a phrase five hundred times as punishment. Still, he did well in school and got good grades.

From a young age, Groening pursued his creative side. "When I was a kid," he recalls, "my friends and I used to put on puppet shows, make comic books, and I decided that's what I wanted to do, to play in every medium."[75] Television cartoons were a big part of Groening's young life, especially the prime-time animated series, *The Adventures of Rocky and Bullwinkle*. When he was nine years old Groening and a group of friends formed the Creature Club, dedicated to drawing scary cartoons. After discovering he was unable to draw a passable Batman, he settled for creating odd-looking characters, including a bug-eyed bunny named Rotten Rabbit. He also won a writing contest sponsored by the children's magazine *Jack and Jill* by completing a Halloween story.

> "My friends and I used to put on puppet shows, make comic books, and I decided that's what I wanted to do, to play in every medium."[75]
>
> —Matt Groening

By the time he entered Portland's Lincoln High School in 1969, Groening's rebellious temperament and dark humor could be seen in both his cartooning and his writing. Groening became a writer and cartoonist for the school newspaper while also publishing his own underground paper, *The Bilge Rat*. With several friends he formed a group called the Komix Appreciation Klub, which eventually included over one hundred members.

In his senior year, Groening applied to two colleges: prestigious Harvard University in Cambridge, Massachusetts, and The Evergreen State College, a progressive liberal arts institution in Olympia,

Matt Groening loved to sketch and create from an early age. However, his drawing talents were not as sophisticated as some other cartoon artists. Instead of giving up on drawing, he stuck to designing simple, sometimes odd-looking characters, including the Simpson family.

Washington. Turned down by the elite eastern school, Groening headed for Olympia, about 100 miles (161 km) north of Portland.

College

Evergreen, a nontraditional college with no tests, no regular classes, and no grades, seemed ideal for the free-thinking Groening. John Ortved, author of a history of *The Simpsons*, characterized the school as a "hippie college at the height of hippiedom."[76] Challenging himself, Groening studied writing and philosophy under Mark Levensky, one of the college's toughest professors. Groening became editor of the college newspaper, *Cooper Point Journal*, for which he wrote and drew cartoons, satirizing politics and the pomposity of the college's liberal viewpoint. Shortly before Groening graduated, Levensky told him, "You do what you do tolerably well. Now you have to ask yourself: Is it worth doing?"[77] Groening would ask himself that very question numerous times as he struggled to make it in the cartooning business. Ultimately, the answer he came up with was "yes."

Groening's *Life in Hell*, aka Los Angeles

After graduating from Evergreen, Groening, twenty-three years old and full of ambition to become a writer, headed for Los Angeles. His introduction to the city was discouraging: his car broke down on the Hollywood Freeway and the only employment he could find consisted of dead-end jobs. But the city led to his first success as a cartoonist. "*Life in Hell* was inspired by my move to Los Angeles in 1977,"[78] he says. The comic strip began as a self-published book that Groening photocopied and sent to his friends back home to illustrate the horrors of living in Los Angeles. His first professional sale came when he sold a cartoon to *WET*, a trendy magazine. Then in 1980 an alternative newspaper called the *Los Angeles Reader* began running *Life in Hell* as a regular strip. Three years later, twenty papers carried the strip, and Groening was on his way to a professional cartooning career.

Life in Hell features a buck-toothed rabbit named Binky (a more refined version of Groening's earlier Rotten Rabbit); his son Bongo; Binky's girlfriend, Sheba; and a pair of bulbous-nosed, fez-wearing gay characters named Akbar and Jeff. Groening called *Life in Hell* "a crude little comic strip full of alienation, angst, fear and grief, not to mention self-loathing and laughs" with themes of "love, sex, work, death, doom and rabbits."[79] Deborah Caplan, whom Groening met in college, worked with him getting the strip into newspapers, as well as marketing T-shirts, mugs, calendars, and other *Life in Hell* merchandise. In 1987, Groening and Caplan were married. The couple had two children, Homer and Abe, before divorcing in 1999. Groening would remain unmarried until 2011, when he married his long-time girlfriend, Argentinian artist Agustina Picasso.

Life in Hell eventually appeared in 379 papers before Groening ended the strip in 2012. But long before that, one of Groening's drawings made its way to the office of one of Hollywood's hottest television producers. It was the spark that ignited Groening's career in television animation.

The Simpsons Is Born

James L. Brooks produced such hit television sitcoms as *The Mary Tyler Moore Show*, *Cheers*, and *Taxi*. In 1987 Brooks was busy working out the details of a new program he was developing for the Fox Broadcasting Company called *The Tracey Ullman Show*. The show featured comedy sketches starring the versatile actress of the program's title. Brooks wanted to bring the show into and out of commercials with short animated clips called bumpers. The *Life in Hell* cartoon on his office wall made him think of Groening, so he arranged for a meeting with the cartoonist.

The story of the meeting has become a bit of a Hollywood legend. As Groening sat outside Brooks's office waiting to go in, he realized that if Brooks were to use his characters for the *Ullman* show, he would have to give up the rights to those characters. Not willing to lose control of his long-running strip, Groening came up with an alternative. Sketching quickly, he created a whole new animated family within the space of about fifteen minutes. Groening called them the Simpsons and placed them in the fictional town of Springfield. He gave the characters first names from his own family: father Homer, mother Marge (short for his mother's name, Margaret), and daughters Lisa and Maggie. Only for one family member did Groening make up a name, calling the mischievous son Bart, an anagram of "brat."

Brooks liked Groening's concept, and a deal was made. Voice actors were hired, most of whom have remained with *The Simpsons* throughout its run, and the small, independent Klasky Csupo studio was hired to do the animation. *The Tracey Ullman Show* debuted on April 5, 1987, and two weeks later *The Simpsons* appeared on the show in four short vignettes. Running less than two minutes in total, the segments show Homer and Marge putting their children to bed, unintentionally frightening the kids with their good-night pleasantries. It was the world's first look at the utterly dysfunctional Simpson family.

The Simpsons and Pop Culture

When Matt Groening created *The Simpsons*, he produced not just a cartoon but an important observer and critic of pop culture. Journalist Chris Turner, in his book *Planet Simpson: How a Masterpiece Defined a Generation*, discusses the show's cultural impact.

The Simpsons brewed a mix of killer one-off gags, laser-guided social satire, robust character development and pure comedic joy into a potion so intoxicating that it became by far the most important cultural institution of its time: the equal of any single body of work to emerge from our pop-cultural stew in the last century in *any* medium. It was the Beatles *and* the Stones. It was Elvis *and* Chuck Berry. It was that big, that unprecedented, and that important. And it also grew so monumental—so fixed on the cultural map—that it now seems impossible to imagine contemporary pop culture without it.

But the rock 'n' roll metaphor is not quite right. Rock & roll hit with the singular force of an atomic bomb—and was indeed a perfect cultural expression of the massive shift in consciousness rent by the splitting of the atom. *The Simpsons* was more like climate change: it built incrementally, week by week, episode by episode, weaving itself into the cultural landscape slowly but surely until it became a permanent feature, a constant reminder that just beneath the luxurious surface of this prosperous time lurked much uglier truths.

Chris Turner, *Planet Simpson: How a Masterpiece Defined a Generation*. Cambridge, MA: Da Capo, 2004, p. 5.

The Simpsons Begins

No television cartoon had ever had a family quite like the one Groening created. The oafish Homer loves beer and donuts and, disconcertingly, works as a safety inspector at Springfield's nuclear power plant. Marge is a typical stay-at-home mother, exasperated by Homer's and Bart's antics. Intellectual eight-year-old Lisa plays the saxophone and supports liberal causes, while baby Maggie's constant sucking on a pacifier belies her inner intelligence. Bart is a mischievous ten-year-old who hates school, disdains authority, and is prone to spouting such catchphrases as "Eat my shorts!" and "Don't have a cow, man!"

The characters were crudely drawn; the animators at Klasky Csupo simply traced them from Groening's sketches. Both audiences and critics paid the bumpers little attention at first. But their popularity grew, and by the third season of the *Ullman* show, *The Simpsons* had transformed from quick bumpers into longer segments placed between the show's live sketches. That third season was the last for *The Tracey Ullman Show*, as it never attained the ratings necessary to keep it on the air.

> "I designed *The Simpsons* to be a TV series, that was always my secret plan. The idea of putting animated characters on prime time was considered very controversial."[80]
>
> —Matt Groening

With *Ullman* gone, Groening and Brooks wondered whether the networks would be open to *The Simpsons* as a full-length prime-time show. "I designed *The Simpsons* to be a TV series," notes Groening, "That was always my secret plan. The idea of putting animated characters on prime time was considered very controversial."[80] Groening and Brooks put together a seven-minute demonstration reel made up of *Simpsons* shorts and screened it for various network executives. When Barry Diller, the chairman of Fox, suggested doing *The Simpsons* as specials, Brooks replied, "It's a series or nothing."[81] Diller ultimately relented, and Fox's newest prime-time animated show was scheduled to begin airing in the fall of 1989.

Prime-Time Homer

Producing a prime-time show was different than crafting short comedy bumpers. *The Simpsons* had to connect with the adult audience if it had any hope of surviving. "When we went to turn it into a TV series," Groening recalls, "[Brooks] said, 'We have to go for real emotion. We have to know what makes these people tick and we have to feel for them. I want people to forget they're watching a cartoon.'"[82] From its first season, the audience accepted the Simpsons as a real family, albeit one that they might not want to have as neighbors. Groening himself believes in the genuineness of his creation. He says, "I think of the Simpsons as

Now well-known cartoon characters, the Simpson family first appeared in 1987 as filler between sketches, and commercials, on The Tracey Ullman Show. The dysfunctional family unit was so popular with audiences that the Fox network gave them their own show two years later.

real, individual people. . . . What drives the Simpsons in general, which I find particularly funny, is their urgent struggle to be normal, whatever that is, and then failing at it every step of the way."[83]

The Simpsons became one of the top-rated shows on Fox. In 1997 it won a Peabody Award for "providing exceptional animation and stinging satire."[84] In 2007 Homer and his family hit the big screen in The Simpsons Movie, which Groening produced and cowrote. Amid critical and audience acclaim, the film made over $500 million worldwide. Groening has made a fortune with The Simpsons, but the show has him pondering his youth. "I think about being 10 years old now," he says, "and watching The Simpsons because I know if I'd seen The Simpsons as a kid, it would've been my favorite show."[85]

Living Creatively

Although he looks like an adult, Matt Groening is still a kid at heart. In an interview with his grammar-school friend Jamie Angell in *Simpsons Illustrated* magazine, Groening gives advice on creative living, which is applicable to adults and kids alike.

Most grown-ups forget what it was like to be a kid. I vowed that I would never forget. I also found child's play—stuff that was not considered serious, but goofy—was the stuff I liked to do, so I still do it as an adult. Living creatively is really important to maintain throughout your life. And living creatively doesn't mean only artistic creativity, although that's part of it. It means being yourself, not just complying with the wishes of other people. The dismal reality is that a lot of people have to work at crummy jobs that they don't want to do. But even if you have a crummy job, you have to save a part of yourself, maybe a secret part, and do the things you want, so that you can be yourself. I'd like to think that's one of the hidden messages of *The Simpsons*. It's a show about people who don't know that secret, but the making of the show is an example of that secret. Sometimes people get mad at *The Simpsons'* subversive storytelling, but there's another message in there, which is a celebration of making wild, funny stories.

Quoted in Jamie Angell, "Explaining Groening—One on One with the Sultan of Fun," *Simpsons Illustrated*, Summer 1993. www.simpsonsarchive.com.

Into the Future

With *The Simpsons* secure in its prime-time slot, Fox wanted Groening to create another animated series for the network. A fan of science fiction since his youth, Groening teamed up with *Simpsons* writer David X. Cohen in 1996 to create *Futurama*, an animated sci-fi series set in the thirtieth century. Early on, Groening described the show as "basically a spiffy, epic future history that's going to honor and satirize the conventions of science fiction in the guise of a little prime-time cartoon show."[86] Taking classic science fiction stories as inspiration, Groening and Cohen's show follows the adventures of Philip J. Fry, a twentieth-century pizza delivery boy who wakes up a thousand years in the future after being accidentally frozen in a state of suspended animation. In his new future world he meets, among many others, the beautiful alien girl Leela and a bad-tempered robot named Bender. *Futurama's* character design is easily recognizable as Simpsons-like, as is Groening's wry view of human nature. "My gut instinct," he comments, "says that in the future, people will still be stupid."[87]

Futurama debuted on March 28, 1999, and ran five seasons on Fox before being canceled for low ratings. *Futurama* reruns appeared on Comedy Central, and four *Futurama* movies were produced for direct-to-video distribution. After being revived for two more seasons on Comedy Central, the show was permanently canceled in 2013. It was revived one last time in November 2014, in a crossover episode of *The Simpsons* in which Fry, Leela, and Bender travel back in time to avert a future crisis caused by, to no one's surprise, Bart.

The Groening Legacy

Groening's career has earned him twelve Emmy Awards, a Reuben Award, a star on Hollywood's Walk of Fame, and a net worth estimated at $500 million. Sharing his good fortune, he donated $500,000 to the UCLA School of Theater, Film and Television, in addition to a $50,000 annual gift to the school to promote socially conscious student animated films. Not everyone gets to impact culture the way Groening's creations have. A measure of that impact is the fact that Homer Simpson's exasperated exclamation, "D'oh!" has been added to the Oxford English Dictionary, and in 2012, the US Postal Service issued stamps featuring *The Simpsons* characters.

> "I think about being 10 years old now and watching *The Simpsons* because I know if I'd seen *The Simpsons* as a kid, it would've been my favorite show."[85]
>
> —*Matt Groening*

Considering his discouraging start in Los Angeles, Groening takes his success with a bit of wit. "Being rewarded for what I used to be discouraged from doing," he says, "is probably the best revenge of all. If I hadn't lucked out, maybe I'd be in a straitjacket."[88] Even in that unlikely scenario, Groening would surely find a way to draw new cartoons.

CHAPTER 6

Aaron McGruder

African Americans have been featured on television sitcoms since the 1950s, when a program called *Amos 'n' Andy* moved from radio to TV. Black families, which were represented by crude stereotypes on *Amos 'n' Andy*, eventually became more realistic in such shows as *The Bill Cosby Show*, *Family Matters*, and *black-ish*, among many others.

As live-action sitcoms have become more true to life, their animated counterparts stretch reality to the breaking point, and sometimes beyond. *The Cleveland Show*, airing from 2009 to 2013, took its style of humor from *Family Guy* and its creator Seth MacFarlane. But even before *The Cleveland Show* made its appearance on television, another show, *The Boondocks*, had been crossing the boundaries of sitcom humor to the anger of its many critics. The show had its roots in a controversial comic strip of the same name, created by a brash young African American cartoonist named Aaron McGruder.

Early Years

Aaron Vincent McGruder was born in Chicago, Illinois, on May 29, 1974. In the late 1970s, the McGruder family, including Aaron; his parents, Bill and Elaine; and his older brother, Dedric, moved several times, finally settling in Columbia, Maryland. There, his father took a job with the National Transportation Safety Board. Columbia was a mostly white, middle-class suburban community, and living there forced McGruder to begin thinking about his black identity. "As a black kid in the suburbs," he remembers, "you had two choices: emphasize your blackness or blend in with the white kids."[89] This conflict would become the basis for *The Boondocks*, a comic strip about black kids living in a white world.

McGruder attended a Jesuit school for grades seven through nine before entering the racially diverse Oakland Mills High School. Hanging out with other black youth for the first time, he became fascinated with hip-hop culture, listening to such groups as Public Enemy and X Clan. Other things that made an impression on the young McGruder were kung-fu movies, video games, and, especially, *Star Wars*. He had begun drawing as a child, and by his teenage years, he knew he wanted to be a cartoonist. McGruder lists the comic strips *Bloom County*, *Doonesbury*, and *Calvin and Hobbes* as influencing his growing social and political awareness.

> "As a black kid in the suburbs you had two choices: emphasize your blackness or blend in with the white kids."[89]
>
> —*Aaron McGruder*

College and *The Boondocks*

After high school McGruder enrolled at the University of Maryland in College Park, where he majored in African American studies. His political and cultural leanings began to emerge in the form of comics. "I wanted to have a way to say something," he recalls. "I wanted a TV show, but realized, 'They're not going to just give away a TV show. Let me do a strip.'"[90] His first idea was to work as a comic book illustrator. After his freshman year at Maryland, McGruder took a year off to try to break into the comic book business. He approached Milestone Media, an African American–owned company publishing comic books featuring black superheroes. Despite impressing the company with his talent, McGruder's work did not fit in with Milestone's comics. "What Aaron brought to us in 1994 was very funny," recalls Dwayne McDuffie, cofounder of Milestone, "but we were doing an action adventure comic. He's just a stunningly talented guy. . . . Besides that, he's fearless."[91]

Giving up his idea of a career in comic books, McGruder returned to the university. While working in the school's Presentation Graphics Laboratory, he created his breakthrough comic strip, *The Boondocks*. Taking a cue from McGruder's own childhood, the two main characters in *The Boondocks* moved from inner-city Chicago to the fictional white suburb of Woodcrest. The strip takes its title from the word *boondocks*, a slang term for a place that is far away from an urban area, somewhere in the middle of nowhere. The comic's family, the Freemans, is not the typical suburban household, consisting of Huey, a ten-year-old black radical; his eight-year-old thug-wannabe brother, Riley; and their legal guardian and grandfather, Robert "Granddad" Freeman. According to McGruder, the Freemans symbolize "three different facets of the angry-black-man archetype."[92] Other characters include Huey's friend Caesar, cantankerous old Uncle Ruckus, and interracial couple Tom and Sarah Dubois and their daughter, Jazmine.

> "What Aaron brought to us in 1994 was very funny. . . . He's just a stunningly talented guy. . . . Besides that, he's fearless."[91]
>
> —Dwayne McDuffie, Milestone Media.

The Boondocks first appeared on the website The Hotlist Online in February 1996. Later that year, McGruder met Jayson Blair, editor in chief of the University of Maryland's independent student newspaper, the *Diamondback*. Blair was looking to add a new strip to the paper and hired McGruder for the job. When *The Boondocks* debuted in the paper in December, it quickly gained an appreciative following among the students. And McGruder was making money from his cartooning: He was paid $30 for each installment, more than double what the other cartoonists in the paper were earning. But the strip had a short life in the *Diamondback*. Due to a technical error in early 1997, *The Boondocks* did not appear in its usual spot, the word "OOPS!" printed in its place. When the editor failed to issue an apology for the error, McGruder pulled his comic; the last strip appeared on March 18, 1997.

Aaron McGruder began drawing his comic strip The Boondocks in 1996 when he was only twenty-two years old. McGruder moved the comic around from the Internet to a student newspaper before it was picked up for national syndication in 1999.

McGruder found another outlet for *The Boondocks* in a hip-hop magazine called the *Source*, but the possibility of reaching a wider audience remained elusive. Then a chance meeting at a convention in Chicago changed McGruder's life forever.

The Boondocks Goes National

At the annual convention of the National Association of Black Journalists, McGruder met Harriet Choice, vice president at Universal Press Syndicate. She was seeking new talent for possible syndication, and McGruder gave her some sample *Boondock*s strips. Choice remembers the encounter:

> I sat in on this meeting of blacks who wanted to be syndicated in comics. I was listening and looking, and all of a sudden, this young man sitting behind me passes something over my shoulders and here's "The Boondocks." . . . I was absolutely blown away.[93]

63

Choice showed the strips to Universal Press editorial director Lee Salem, who agreed that McGruder had something special and drew up a syndication contract for *The Boondocks*. When the strip went national in April 1999, it appeared in 160 newspapers, the largest debut of any comic strip in history. At the time there were only two widely circulated comic strips featuring black characters and drawn by African American cartoonists. *The Boondocks* stood out from the others with its controversial language and content and a visual style that McGruder took from Japanese manga. In the beginning, Huey and Riley are concerned with how to cope with the radical change in their lives after moving from inner city to outer suburb. In one early panel, Riley asks Huey as they walk through their new neighborhood, "What is that smell?" Huey replies, "Clean air. My guess is we'll get used to it eventually."[94] In another strip, when Riley suggests that the boys steal a Lexus and return to Chicago, Huey rejects the idea: "Forget it, Riley. We're stuck here."[95]

By 2000 *The Boondocks* was appearing in some 300 newspapers, and McGruder was now well-off due to his six-figure syndication contract. But success had its price. He had moved to Los Angeles in late 1999, leaving behind familiar surroundings and making his solitary life as a cartoonist even lonelier. Dealing with constant deadlines was also starting to wear on McGruder's health. On a visit to see his family in Maryland in the spring of 2000, he was hospitalized with severe gastrointestinal pain caused by the stress he was under. "I was in so much agony, I couldn't work," he recalls. "I mean, it was physically killing me because it was too much."[96] Doctors warned him that if he did not make changes in his stressful life, he would die. McGruder's health began to improve when he reconciled himself to the fact that occasionally missing a deadline would not mean the end of his career.

In the early years of *The Boondocks,* McGruder concentrated on developing his characters and sharpening his humor rather than making political statements. That all changed on September 11, 2001.

The Boondocks After 9/11

The terrorist attacks that day on the World Trade Center in New York City and the Pentagon near Washington, DC, brought the

Aaron McGruder's Comic Book

When comic book publisher Milestone Media turned down Aaron McGruder's work, he decided that he was through with comic books and would concentrate instead on his comic strip *The Boondocks*. But a funny thing happened later in McGruder's career: Ten years after his rejection, he became the coauthor of a comic book.

Birth of a Nation is a graphic novel cowritten by McGruder and Reginald Hudlin, his producing partner on *The Boondocks* animated television series. African American artist Kyle Baker drew the comic in a movie storyboard-like format, with Hudlin and McGruder's dialogue appearing beneath the panels. The book is a social satire based on an intriguing premise: What if the mostly African American city of East St. Louis, Illinois, seceded from the United States? When citizens of East St. Louis are prevented from voting in a presidential election, Mayor Fred Fredericks leads the city in leaving the United States and forming the independent Republic of Blackland. *Birth of a Nation* skewers social and cultural problems while providing a scathing commentary on America's controversial election of 2000. Texas governor George W. Bush won that election amid cries of vote fraud; in *Birth of a Nation*, the president is a barely disguised Bush.

Birth of a Nation was hailed by many as a brilliant satire on race relations. But another brilliant move was the naming of the book: the title was taken from a 1915 silent movie that glorified the racism of the Ku Klux Klan.

nation together in a state of shock, fear, and mourning. American flags flew with new prominence across the country, and newspapers lauded America's renewed patriotism and solidarity. For McGruder, however, something seemed wrong with the nation and its leader, President George W. Bush:

> I started seeing a problem. Journalists stopped being journalists. All this cheerleading started. All of a sudden this lame president was being hailed as a bold national leader. No one was asking questions about how every system designed to protect this country failed. And where were all these flags coming from? I was disgusted by the whole thing. . . . I suddenly knew what I wanted to do. And the material just wrote itself. It was then I became a political cartoonist.[97]

McGruder began criticizing the new patriotism and the Bush administration in his strip. He created strips featuring two new characters, Flagee and Ribbon, which replaced the regular *Boondocks* installments. Flagee, an American flag, and Ribbon, a yellow ribbon, mocked the nation's growing display of patriotism after the 9/11 attacks. McGruder especially targeted President Bush, who in one strip is called "the dumbest man alive."[98] In a Thanksgiving Day *Boondocks* strip in 2001, McGruder compared the president to Osama bin Laden. Several newspapers temporarily pulled *The Boondocks*, noting that while views like those expressed in the strip were welcome on the editorial pages, the comic section was not the appropriate place for them.

Offending Nearly Everyone

Politicians were not the only people ridiculed by McGruder. He took African American celebrities, including Cuba Gooding Jr, Sean "Puffy" Combs, and Vivica A. Fox, to task for what he felt was their demeaning of black culture. One of his most frequent targets was Black Entertainment Television (BET) and its founder, Robert L. Johnson, whom he accused of perpetuating racial stereotypes in the interest of keeping advertisers happy. Johnson responded to McGruder's criticism by saying that "the 500 dedicated employees of BET do more in one day to serve the interests of African-Americans than this young man has done in his entire life."[99] Many institutions, such as the National Rifle Association, the American news media, and even Santa Claus, also felt the sting of McGruder's satirical jabs.

By 2004 McGruder's busy life and the stress of trying to meet relentless deadlines threatened to take a toll on the strip. He hired an artist to produce the artwork of *The Boondocks*, while he concentrated on the writing, a job he felt he was better at than drawing. In March 2006 *The Boondocks* took a six-month hiatus to give McGruder a chance to recharge his creative batteries and develop fresh ideas for the strip. But a return to the newspa-

In 2005, The Boondocks *was transplanted from print to television, airing on the Cartoon Network for nine years. During its fifty-five-episode run, the show, like the strip, confronted issues of race, civil rights, and identity while telling the story of a black family living in a white suburb.*

pers was not to be. Lee Salem of Universal Press Syndicate announced in September 2006 that McGruder had decided to end *The Boondocks*. Salem left the door open for future installments should McGruder decide to revive the strip.

After ten years of satirizing politics and patriotism, movie stars and media moguls, *The Boondocks* quietly slipped into comic strip history. But McGruder was not finished with Huey, Riley, and the other residents of Woodcrest.

The Boondocks on Television

As early as 1998 McGruder had begun working with film producer Reginald Hudlin to create a *Boondocks* TV show. The Fox

Red Tails

In 1988, George Lucas had an idea for a movie filled with aerial combat and brave heroes. It did not feature Jedi knights, however, but a group of African American World War II aviators known as the Tuskegee Airmen. Their all-black squadron was called the Red Tails, after the crimson color of the tails of their fighter planes, and they distinguished themselves in more than fifteen hundred combat missions. In 2010 Lucas produced *Red Tails*, his film about the Tuskegee Airmen.

When George Lucas asks a person to be a writer on one of his films, the answer is almost certainly a resounding "yes." Principal photography had already finished when Lucas hired Aaron McGruder to help create dialogue for additional scenes in post-production. As filmed, *Red Tails* was a serious historical drama but, Lucas felt, perhaps a bit too serious. McGruder worked at Lucas's Skywalker Ranch, where his role gradually grew larger as Lucas incorporated many of his creative ideas into the movie. For example, he helped create action scenes that young viewers had come to expect from a George Lucas film.

McGruder, whose father was a military pilot, says that the Tuskegee Airmen have been his heroes throughout his life and that *Red Tails* gave them a long-overdue exposure. "One of the last things I said to George was: 'This movie kind of represents the last barrier of equality for the black fighting man. We've never had the John Wayne treatment.'" McGruder helped make that treatment become a reality.

Quoted in Bryan Curtis, "George Lucas Is Ready to Roll the Credits," *New York Times Magazine*, January 17, 2012. www.nytimes.com.

network rejected a pilot episode in 2003, but the show finally found a home in the Cartoon Network's *Adult Swim* late night programming block. Like its print forerunner, the animated *Boondocks* spared no one from its satirical barbs. In its first episode, Huey says Jesus is black, former president Ronald Reagan the devil, and the 9/11 attacks a government conspiracy. Such dialogue, with numerous instances of the "n-word" and frequent use of expletives, set the tone for the entire series.

The show also presented a bold alternate-history episode in which Dr. Martin Luther King Jr., wounded but not killed by an assassin in 1968, awakes from a coma after thirty-two years and voices his disgust with the way black culture has evolved. A statement from the Cartoon Network about the controversial episode said, "We think Aaron McGruder came up with a thought-provoking way of not only showing Dr. King's bravery but also of reminding us of what he stood and fought for."[100] The episode received harsh criticism from civil rights activist the Reverend Al Sharpton, but it also won a prestigious Peabody Award.

A total of fifty-five episodes of *The Boondocks* series aired on *Adult Swim* from its debut in 2005 to its final episode in 2014. It brought Huey and his family to life and introduced them to a new audience of young people who had never seen the strip in its print version.

Now in his forties, McGruder has not lost the edge that made *The Boondocks* a successful critic of society as seen through the eyes of two radical African American children. In the summer of 2014 he launched another television program, a live-action sitcom entitled *Black Jesus*. Debuting on *Adult Swim* to an audience of over two million viewers, the series finds Jesus living in present-day Compton, California, smoking marijuana, and cursing with abandon while spreading the Gospel and doing good in the 'hood. Not surprisingly, Christian groups blasted *Black Jesus* for mocking the Christian religion, and some advertisers pulled their commercials from the show. Executive producer Robert Eric Wise defends the show's portrayal of Jesus, noting that "what Aaron has done, and I feel this in my heart—he's made Jesus cool."[101]

> "What Aaron has done, and I feel this in my heart—he's made Jesus cool."[101]
>
> —Robert Eric Wise, executive producer, Black Jesus.

Whether he is seen as cool or controversial, McGruder remains unafraid to speak his mind with his art, on paper or on television. As a celebrity he keeps a low personal profile, but he is comfortable with his own success. "At the end of the day," he muses, "there's nothing like being an articulate, intelligent person who knows who they are and where they came from."[102]

SOURCE NOTES

Introduction: The Art of the Cartoonist

1. Quoted in Laurence Maslon, *Superheroes!: Capes, Cowls, and the Creation of Comic Book Culture*. New York: Crown, 2013, p. 17.
2. James Billington, foreword to *Cartoon America: Comics in the Library of Congress*, ed. Harry Katz. New York: Abrams, 2006, p.7.

Chapter 1: Charles Schulz

3. Quoted in Rheta Grimsley Johnson, *Good Grief: The Story of Charles M. Schulz*. New York: Pharos, 1989, p. 17.
4. Quoted in David Michaelis, *Schulz and Peanuts: A Biography*. New York: HarperCollins, 2007, p. 55.
5. Quoted in David Michaelis, "Charles Schulz," Chuck Jones Official Website. www.chuckjones.com.
6. Charles M. Schulz, *My Life with Charlie Brown*. Jackson: University Press of Mississippi, 2010, p. 7.
7. Quoted in Schulz, *My Life with Charlie Brown*, p. 12.
8. Quoted in Michaelis, *Schulz and Peanuts*, p. 129.
9. Quoted in Schulz, *My Life with Charlie Brown*, p. 17.
10. Quoted in Chip Kidd, *Only What's Necessary: Charles M. Schulz and the Art of Peanuts*. New York: Abrams, 2015, p. 16.
11. Quoted in Michaelis, *Schulz and Peanuts*, p. 209.
12. Quoted in Michaelis, *Schulz and Peanuts*, p. 221.
13. Charles M. Schulz, *Peanuts: A Golden Celebration; The Art and the Story of the World's Best-Loved Comic Strip*. New York: HarperCollins, 1999, p. 15.

14. Garry Trudeau, "'I Hate Charlie Brown': An Appreciation," in *Charles M. Schulz: Conversations,* M. Thomas Inge, ed. Jackson: University Press of Mississippi, 2000, p. 271.
15. Schulz, *My Life with Charlie Brown*, p. 13.
16. Quoted in Kidd, *Only What's Necessary*.
17. Quoted in Johnson, *Good Grief*, p. 86.
18. Quoted in Sarah Boxer, "The Exemplary Narcissism of Snoopy," *The Atlantic*, November, 2015, p. 108.
19. Quoted in Beverly Gherman, *Sparky: The Life and Art of Charles Schulz*. San Francisco: Chronicle, 2010, pp. 117–18.

Chapter 2: Garry Trudeau

20. G.B. Trudeau, *The Long Road Home: One Step at a Time*. Kansas City, MO: Andrews McMeel, 2005, p. 11.
21. Quoted in Brian Walker, *Doonesbury and the Art of G.B. Trudeau*. New Haven, CT: Yale University Press, 2010, p. 4.
22. Quoted in Walker, *Doonesbury and the Art of G.B. Trudeau*, p. 5.
23. Quoted in Walker, *Doonesbury and the Art of G.B. Trudeau*, p. 5.
24. G.B. Trudeau, *40: A Doonesbury Retrospective*. Kansas City, MO: Andrews McMeel, 2005, p. 8.
25. *Washington Post,* "GB Trudeau's Doonesbury: The Yale Strips." http://doonesbury.washingtonpost.com.
26. Quoted in Walker, *Doonesbury and the Art of G.B. Trudeau*, p. 7.
27. Quoted in Walker, *Doonesbury and the Art of G.B. Trudeau*, p. 11.
28. Quoted in Jonathan Alter, "Real Life with Garry Trudeau," *Newsweek*, October 15, 1990, p. 60.
29. Quoted in G.B. Trudeau, *Flashbacks: 25 Years of Doonesbury*. Kansas City, MO: Andrews McMeel, 1995, p. 9.
30. *Doonesbury*, October 26, 1970. http://doonesbury.washingtonpost.com
31. Trudeau, *40: A Doonesbury Retrospective*, p. 45.
32. Quoted in Kerry D. Soper, *Garry Trudeau: Doonesbury and the Aesthetics of Satire*. Jackson: University of Mississippi Press, 2008, p. 73.
33. Quoted in G.B. Trudeau, *Flashbacks*, p. 39.
34. Quoted in Walker, *Doonesbury and the Art of G.B. Trudeau,* p. 21.
35. G.B. Trudeau, *Flashbacks*, p. 166.
36. Quoted in Eric Bates, "Doonesbury Goes to War," *Rolling Stone*, August 5, 2004. www.timemachinego.com.
37. G.B. Trudeau, *Flashbacks*, p. 234.

38. Garry Trudeau, speech at George Polk Awards ceremony, April 10, 2015, in "The Abuse of Satire," *Atlantic*, April 11, 2015. www .theatlantic.com.

39. Garry Trudeau interview on *Meet the Press*, NBC News, April 25, 2015. www.nbcnews.com.

40. G.B. Trudeau: *Flashbacks*, p. 322.

Chapter 3: Lynn Johnston

41. Lynn Johnston and Katherine Hadway, *For Better or For Worse: The Comic Art of Lynn Johnston*. Fredericton, New Brunswick, Canada: Goose Lane, 2015, p. 25.

42. Johnston and Hadway, *For Better or For Worse*, p. 27.

43. Johnston and Hadway, *For Better or For Worse*, p. 54.

44. Lynn Johnston, *A Look Inside . . . For Better or For Worse: The 10th Anniversary Collection*. Kansas City, MO: Andrews McMeel, 1989, p. 45.

45. Johnston and Hadway, *For Better or For Worse*, p. 89.

46. Quoted in Bob Andelman, "Universal Press Syndicate Editor Lee Salem on Funny Pages! Interview," February 27, 2007. www.mr media.com.

47. Johnston and Hadway, *For Better or For Worse*, p. 106.

48. Johnston, *A Look Inside*, p. 58.

49. Lynn Johnston, *Suddenly Silver: Celebrating 25 Years of For Better or For Worse*. Kansas City, MO: Andrews McMeel, 2004, p. 4.

50. Lynn Johnston, "Lawrence's Story," *For Better or For Worse*. www .fborfw.com.

51. Johnston, "Lawrence's Story."

52. Johnston and Hadway, *For Better or For Worse*, p. 131.

53. *For Better or For Worse*, August 31, 2008.

54. Johnston and Hadway, *For Better or For Worse*, p. 14.

Chapter 4: Seth MacFarlane

55. Seth MacFarlane, "Seth MacFarlane: TV's 'Family Guy' Makes Music, Too," *Fresh Air*, October 17, 2011. www.npr.org.

56. MacFarlane, "Seth MacFarlane: TV's 'Family Guy.'"

57. Quoted in Claire Hoffman, "No. 1 Offender," *New Yorker*, June 18, 2012. www.newyorker.com.

58. Quoted in "Seth MacFarlane," Biography.com. www.biography .com.

59. Seth MacFarlane on "Inside the Actors Studio," Bravo network, September 14, 2009.

60. Quoted in Dan Snierson, "'Simpsons' and 'Family Guy' Creators Matt Groening and Seth MacFarlane Talk Crossover Episode, Movies, Rivalry," *Entertainment Weekly*, September 27, 2014. www.ew.com.

61. Quoted in Lacey Rose, "Seth MacFarlane: The Restless Mind of a Complicated Cartoonist," *Hollywood Reporter*, October 12, 2011. www.hollywoodreporter.com.

62. IGN, "An Interview with Seth MacFarlane: The Creator of *Family Guy* Discusses His Career," July 21, 2003. www.ign.com.

63. IGN, "An Interview with Seth MacFarlane."

64. Quoted in Bernard Weinraub, "The Young Guy Of 'Family Guy'; A 30-Year-Old's Cartoon Hit Makes An Unexpected Comeback," *New York Times*, July 7, 2004. www.nytimes.com.

65. Quoted on *CBS Sunday Morning*, "Q & A with Seth MacFarlane," *CBS Sunday Morning*, February 5, 2013. www.cbsnews.com.

66. Quoted in Internet Movie Database, "Rachael MacFarlane: Biography." www.imdb.com.

67. Parents Television Council, "Family Guide to Prime Time Television: *Family Guy*." www.parentstv.org.

68. Quoted in Amid Amidi, "The John Kricfalusi Interview, Part 2," Cartoon Brew. www.cartoonbrew.com.

69. Quoted in Jonah Weiner, "Q&A: Seth MacFarlane on Hosting the Oscars, Being Hated by 'South Park,'" *Rolling Stone*, December 11, 2012. www. rollingstone.com.

70. Quoted in Kimberly Nordyke and Bryn Elise Sandberg, "The 'Family Guy' Creator Received the Genius Award on Sunday Night," *Hollywood Reporter*, May 31, 2015. www.hollywoodreporter.com.

71. Quoted in Steve Pond, "Seth MacFarlane: Thoughts on the Once (and Future?) Oscar Host," *Wrap*, April 22, 2013. www.thewrap.com.

72. Quoted in Max Nicholson, "Comic-Con 2015: What's Next for *Family Guy* and *American Dad*?," IGN, July 11, 2015. www.ign.com.

Chapter 5: Matt Groening

73. Quoted in Tim Delaney, *Simpsonology: There's a Little Bit of Springfield in All of Us.* Amherst, NY: Prometheus, 2008, p. 27.

74. Quoted in Susan G. Hauser, "Mr. Groening's Neighborhood," *Wall Street Journal*, October 7, 1999. www.wsj.com.

75. Quoted in Elizabeth Kolbert, "AT WORK WITH: Matt Groening; The Fun of Being Bart's Real Dad," *New York Times*, February 25, 1993. www.nytimes.com.

76. John Ortved, *The Simpsons: An Uncensored, Unauthorized History*. New York: Faber & Faber, 2009, p. 14.

77. Quoted in Dick Anderson, "Every Picture Tells a Story," *Evergreen Magazine*, Spring 2012, The Evergreen State College. www.evergreen.edu.

78. Quoted in Ortved, *The Simpsons*, p. 15.

79. Quoted in Paul Andrews, "The Groening of America—'Simpsons' Creator Started Jabbing at Life's Lessons During His Days at Evergreen," *Seattle Times*, August 19, 1990. http://community.seattletimes.nwsource.com.

80. Quoted in Ortved, *The Simpsons*, p. 75.

81. Quoted in Ortved, *The Simpsons*, p. 74.

82. Matt Groening and James L. Brooks, interview with Charlie Rose, July 30, 2007, quoted in Ortved, *The Simpsons*, p. 81.

83. Quoted in Joe Morganstern, "Bart Simpson's Real Father: Recalling the Fear and Absurdity of Childhood, Matt Groening Has Created a Cartoon Sitcom More Human than Most Live-Action Shows," *Los Angeles Times*, April 29, 1990. www.latimes.com.

84. Quoted in Chris Turner, *Planet Simpson: How a Cartoon Masterpiece Defined a Generation*. Cambridge, MA: Da Capo, 2004, p. 39.

85. Quoted in Morganstern, "Bart Simpson's Real Father."

86. Quoted in Brian Doherty, "Matt Groening," *Mother Jones*, March/April 1999. www.motherjones.com.

87. Quoted in Alex Needham, "Nice Planet . . . We'll Take It!," *Face*, October 1999. www.archive.org.

88. Quoted in Ellen Warren and Terry Armour, "Film Critics Here Look for Promise on 'Dance' Set," *Chicago Tribune*, January 25, 2000. www.chicagotribune.com.

Chapter Six: Aaron McGruder

89. Quoted in Stephanie Kang, "Down in the *Boondocks*: Cartoonist Aaron McGruder," *Los Angeles Magazine*, August 1, 2001, reprinted in Aaron McGruder, *All the Rage: The Boondocks Past and Present*. New York: Three Rivers, 2007, p. 138.

90. Quoted in R.C. Harvey, "Encountering Aaron McGruder," *Comics Journal*, September 2003, reprinted in McGruder, *All the Rage*, p. 167.

91. Quoted in Michael Datcher, "Free Huey: Aaron McGruder's Outer Child Is Taking on America," in *Crisis*, September/October 2003, p. 42.

92. Quoted in Ben McGrath, "The Radical: Why Do Editors Keep Throwing 'The Boondocks' Off the Funnies Page?," *New Yorker*, April 19, 2004. www.newyorker.com.

93. Quoted in Lonnae O'Neal Parker, "Funnies Man," *Washington Post*, April 26, 1999. www.washingtonpost.com.

94. *The Boondocks*, April 20, 1999, *GOCOMICS*. www.gocomics .com.

95. *The Boondocks*, April 26, 1999, *GOCOMICS*. www.gocomics .com.

96. Quoted in Harvey, "Encountering Aaron McGruder," p. 166.

97. Quoted in Greg Braxton, "He's Gotta Fight the Powers That Be," *Los Angeles Times*, April 25, 2004. www.latimes.com.

98. *The Boondocks*, November 6, 2000. *GOCOMICS*. www.gocom ics.com.

99. Quoted in John Simpkins, "The Equal-Opportunity Offender: Aaron McGruder's 'Boondocks' Is the Anti-'Family Circus,'" *New York Times Magazine*, June 24, 2001. www.nytimes.com.

100. Quoted in DeWayne Wickham, "'Boondocks' Steps over Line in Its Treatment of King," *USA Today*, January 31, 2006. www.usa today.com.

101. Quoted in David Bienenstock, "Black Jesus Has Risen: The Gospel According to Aaron McGruder," *Vice*, August 7, 2014. www .vice.com.

102. Quoted in Kang, "Down in the *Boondocks*," in McGruder, *All the Rage*, p. 139.

FOR FURTHER RESEARCH

Books
Lynn Johnston and Katherine Hadway, *For Better or For Worse: The Comic Art of Lynn Johnston*. Fredericton, New Brunswick, Canada: Goose Lane, 2015.

Stuart A. Kallen, *Matt Groening and "The Simpsons."* San Diego, CA: ReferencePoint Press, 2016.

Charles M. Schulz, *My Life with Charlie Brown*. Jackson: University Press of Mississippi, 2010.

Gail Snyder, *Seth MacFarlane and "Family Guy."* San Diego, CA: ReferencePoint Press, 2016.

Brian Walker, *"Doonesbury" and the Art of G.B. Trudeau*. New Haven, CT: Yale University Press, 2010.

Internet Sources
Bob Andelman, "Universal Press Syndicate Editor Lee Salem on Funny Pages! Interview," Mr. Media, February 22, 2007. http://mrmedia.com/2007/02/universal-press-syndicate-editor-lee-salem-funny-pages-interview/#.Vrztyeb4Pcs.

Ben McGrath, "The Radical: Why Do Editors Keep Throwing 'The Boondocks' Off the Funnies Page?," *New Yorker*, April 19, 2004. www.newyorker.com/magazine/2004/04/19/the-radical.

Ken P., "An Interview with Seth MacFarlane: The Creator of *Family Guy* Discusses His Career," IGN, July 21, 2003. www.ign.com/articles/2003/07/21/an-interview-with-seth-macfarlane.

Garry Trudeau, "Behind the Lines: *Doonesbury* Cartoonist Pulls Duty Getting to Know Soldiers and Their Problems to Make Strip Authentic," SFGate, October 23, 2005. www.sfgate.com/opinion/article/Behind -the-lines-Doonesbury-cartoonist-pulls-2563812.php.

Websites

***The Boondocks* Fan Site** (www.boondocks.net).This site is dedicated to *The Boondocks* animated television show, with a synopsis of each episode, detailed character biographies, and information on *The Boondocks* compilation books.

Charles M. Schulz Museum (www.schulzmuseum.org). The official website of Schulz's museum contains a biography and timeline of the cartoonist, information on exhibits and artifacts, and a blog by Jean Schulz, Sparky's widow.

***For Better or For Worse* Official Website** (www.fborfw.com). This website is loaded with an archive of almost all FBorFW strips, detailed biographies of the main characters, games, podcasts, and a behind-the-scenes look at how the strip was created.

G.B. Trudeau's *Doonesbury* (http://doonesbury.washingtonpost .com). Hosted by the *Washington Post* newspaper, this site includes current and archived strips, a daily news briefing, videos, games, and "The Sandbox," a forum for current service members and veterans.

Simpsoncrazy (www.simpsoncrazy.com). The ultimate website for fans who are crazy about *The Simpsons.* An episode guide, sample show scripts, games, an image gallery, and reviews of *Simpsons* episodes are just some of the site's massive content.

INDEX

78